AN AU

AN AUTISTIC SUN

Christopher's University Challenge

Mike Thorpe

Not a book about autism.
A book about a boy who just
happens to be autistic.

Helianthus

British Library Cataloguing in Publication Data
A catalogue record for this book is available from the British Library.

ISBN 978-1-9164888-0-9

Typeset by Amolibros, Milverton, Somerset, www.amolibros.co.uk
This book production has been managed by Amolibros
Printed and bound by Lightning Source

The author wishes to record his sincere appreciation for the generous and valued support of author and broadcaster Liam Nolan during compilation of this work.

To all those who have come into contact with Chris, whenever, wherever, and to what degree during his life offering support, interest, concern, encouragement and more.

    …thank you.

The love of a mother who, it must be said, has had more than the odd sleepless night concerning Chris.

    … unconditional.

The many moments of absolute joy with him and to see the staggering development he has made and the progress achieved.

    …priceless.

The extent of the bond of brother with brother.

    …absolute.

Peter,

For friendship.

Mike T.

For Chris
and wherever he may take himself in the future.

Contents

Dad is a retired engineer from the world of Oil, Gas and Petro-Chemicals.

Like any walk of life, an environment fraught with its own peculiar content, challenges and deadlines. Characteristics not so entirely different to those faced by our Chris.

Being close to autism is not a life sentence, merely a different way of experiencing and sharing enlightenment and development. A good life.

PROLOGUE

How do people accommodate changes in their life?

The hope might be that it should be done constructively, compassionately, realistically, with an open mind committed to the concept of the need for support...and sometimes unconditional support at that.

Whether we as a family have done so ourselves is an open question. Some might say that we have learnt to do this over time rather than having started out on our path with that intent. No matter. To accommodate the sort of necessary effort for the scope and impact of significant changes would in any event require a catalyst to provoke that very reason for change.

The answer is of course for each to make up their own mind. If you follow the trails set out in this narrative and have not learnt something from them, not enjoyed the stories nor even occasionally been uplifted by them, then we have failed in our intent.

The book offers observations, explanations and some entreaties regarding the human condition from our perspective. The intent is not to lecture here – not to delve too deeply into the science – rather to say what we have found and done, what we may have failed at, where we have succeeded, what we have not done, as well as to consider what we sometimes might have done.

Efforts have been made to try and avoid what might be construed just a droll blog or a sequential timeline report of events. Rather there is the hope it will be recognised that the individual chapters are more along the lines of narrative features and episodes or events, most with observations, consequences and status. Chronologically then, the content of some of these chapters may necessarily overlap or provide a degree of duplication.

There can be no doubt that our lives have been changed, but from the point of view of where we are today, we would not have had it any other way.

We have not necessarily done everything right or in accordance with perceived thinking (far from it), but we do hope we have constantly and consistently applied ourselves to act with due consideration to the matter in hand. We have done this with our best intentions, the unstinting help of many others along the way and generally with the benefit of a considerable amount of laughter. Humour helps – try it.

That 'matter in hand' in the text is our own Christopher, aka… Chris, or more prosaically …

Our Very Own Catalyst

★★★

Our Own Autistic Son

★★★

Our Own Autistic Sun

CHAPTER ONE

In The Beginning

Dad Born: *30th July 1948*
                                                  (Seems a very long time ago now)
Mum Born: *30th August 1951*
Number #1 Son Born: *8th September 1990*
Number #2 Son Born: *'Work-in-progress'*

Two people as a family living in Surrey in the late 1980s and shortly to become a dad and a mum.

He, an engineer, had waited rather long in life to find the perfect partner and was worrying about that more than he should when, just at the right time, he met the lovely woman who was going to be his wife, partner, lover, soul mate, all-time best friend, trusted confidante and, if they were to be so fortunate, mother to their children.

When young, one can afford to be idealistic. Pragmatism comes with age and the accommodation and accumulation of the impact of life itself. He found himself in the unbelievably fortunate position in his late thirties of having waved goodbye to pragmatism and found his own special person, the person he wanted to spend the rest of his life with. In the vernacular he had got a 'real result'. Thank heavens she seemed to agree.

From her own perspective, she still says today that meeting her man was "like finding the other half of me".

Some accolade that.

She has an insatiable appetite for reading fiction, a strong interest in history (particularly, and separately, social history and the Tudor period), plus an accounting-based career background.

This was to be a very strong relationship which, although freely entered into, was later to be challenged in a number of ways. The brief dip into their backgrounds here is relevant as far as it goes, but this is a book about Christopher.

Marriage came on 11th June 1988.

"Ah, yes – I remember it well!"

They had always been able to talk to each other honestly and earnestly but, just over a year later, the matter of "Shall we, or shall we not?" came up.

Yes, the question was would they try for children? It might be thought irrational that two reasonably level-headed people would get married without having seriously entertained such a matter before the nuptials, but they were very much in love.

Unfettered passion ensued, or rather continued, with the result that a very short time later – in two shakes of a duck's tail feather so to speak – he was presented with the results of a home pregnancy test which proved joyously positive. In due course they were safely and gratefully delivered of number #1 son, (Thomas Edmund Donald Thorpe), who has since grown to be 6' – 7" tall. He remains their first most treasured bundle, although slightly larger now! He is dearly loved and always will be. Having been fortunate enough to discover the fulfilment of having a child, thoughts turned to possibly providing a sibling. Here the tale takes a more sombre turn.

There had been a miscarriage before the arrival of Thomas, but the decision having been made that two children would be even more fun than one, a second pregnancy was rather embarrassingly quickly established…or so it was thought.

By week seven of the pregnancy, it was obvious that something was amiss and a trip to St Peter's Hospital in Chertsey followed hot on the heels of a doctor's referral. Various scans were taken. The diagnosis was that there was no viable pregnancy and that there must have been a very early miscarriage. They were sent home.

A couple of days later, on the Saturday, there were severe stomach cramps which got progressively worse during the course of the evening. An emergency call resulted in an ambulance trip to Frimley Park Hospital, on 'blue lights'.

As is the way of things, by the time she was tucked up in a hospital bed, the pains had reduced. She was examined by a young lady doctor who pronounced the symptoms as nothing worse than bowel gas, although it was decided to keep her in overnight for a pregnancy test on the Monday to make sure all was well.

The pregnancy test came back positive, but as it was the Bank Holiday weekend and there was no radiographic facility available, she was left to cool her heels in her hospital bed, suffering no further pains and reconciled to her favourite pastime of reading books to fill the time. How fortunate this was to turn out to be.

All was soon to change. By late evening the pains had returned with a vengeance and, despite her having taken a sleeping tablet, were so excruciating that she collapsed in the ladies toilet. She was be taken down to theatre for an urgent exploratory examination.

Unfortunately there was already an emergency case in Maternity so she was left waiting, but being checked every fifteen minutes, before finally being rushed down to theatre with no time for the pre-med. To this day, she vividly remembers the operating theatre lights.

At 4 a.m. in the morning the phone rang in the bedroom at home. He had never woken up so fast in his life.

"Sister here. Your wife has just been taken down to theatre for an emergency procedure – everything should be OK."

She continued, "Yes – you can come along at any time." **Aargh!**

As might be imagined, the next few hours passed in a blur, however, it was important to try to keep calm and logical…fat chance! Chilling.

He made it to the hospital to find her in bed in the ward, unconscious but 'in recovery'. Sitting by the bed he was waiting – just waiting. She opened her eyes and smiled.

So, what had happened here? Essentially she had had a ruptured ectopic pregnancy. This is not a particularly rare thing, however, when it occurs, things move very quickly to a conclusion one way or the other. One way involves survival and the other… well, does it have to be spelt out? Without the sort of care and attention she received at the hospital there would have been a loss too large to contemplate.

In time there was, thankfully, full physical recovery though now and again the mind harks back to those dramatic circumstances. This had not just been a single ectopic event but no more and no less than a double ectopic. On his side of the family twins occurred in alternate generations for as long back as could be remembered. There is little doubt that the next twins on his side of the family would now have to wait another couple of generations.

She returned home to find the lamp-post and tree in the front garden covered in yellow ribbons. Now was the time to get back to living, working and rearing Thomas.

A summer break that year saw them on the sandy beach in Weymouth with him as Dad in one deck chair, Thomas (some nine months old) on a towel on the groundsheet and her as Mum in another deck chair, accompanied by one of her books. Says Dad to Mum at the time, eyeing her book with some sense of concern …

"What do you think you are going to do with that then?"

After a two-week holiday, and by her own admission, she had read the grand total of three pages.

CHAPTER TWO

And Then There Were Four

Number #2 Son Born: *27th August 1992*
Named: *Christopher James Michael Thorpe*
                       ...our catalyst!

The knock on the front door was from long-time neighbour and friend Cheryl. She had called by for a chat.

This time he was the one to answer the door, with the timing some six or seven months after the challenges of the ectopic. In finishing the two-way doorstep conversation, she said quietly:

"Do you think you will try for another one?"

A valid question, sensitively put. The answer at the time went something along the lines of:

"I really don't know, she has been through such a lot and although it might be nice to try, I don't really know how she feels about it just now. We just haven't talked about it much. We don't really know the risks involved."

He closed the door with that very thought on his mind.

The grounds were thus laid for another of their periodic deliberations. She started this one off a while later by saying that she had been sorting through some baby clothes upstairs and, without trying to appear too emotional about it, something was telling her that this was not the time to stop. She wanted to try for another baby. It was only then that he mentioned the earlier doorstep exchange.

When decisions were to be made, they would do their usual thing of looking at matters from all perspectives, up, down, inside, outside and sideways, along with consideration of possible consequences and outcomes. Things were no different here for what was agreed to be this one-time-only option. Such conversations normally involved a "why not?" question. Given that this usually led to a yes or no agreement and that, in this case there was no issue with what they had swiftly decided, the next step was to make a doctor's appointment. She was able to see their family doctor, the venerable and highly regarded Dr MacFarlane, at the village practice.

She returned from the surgery with the advice that whilst their body clocks were at the mature stage for procreation, knowing the family as the good doctor did, there was no reason at all not to try again. It had mischievously been said to the doctor that with now only one Fallopian tube left it might take two months to fall pregnant rather than one.

With all due concern for those who have the greatest difficulty in achieving childbirth, it did indeed only take two months for her to fall pregnant again. The thought occurred that "It must be down to something in the water."

As an older prospective mother-to-be, she would commit herself to all appointments, inspections and necessary tests for the duration and, by firm intent, apply herself to the role of model patient. She was a responsible grown-up after all and she would heed all the latest advice (no alcohol, lots of vegetables, a top-up of vitamins and the like). Giving up smoking was fortunately not a problem as nobody in the family smoked.

When expecting a longed-for baby, the anticipation grows. Arrangements are put in place in terms of baby clothes, birth plan, possible names, and, most importantly, preparing cherished existing son for the future exciting arrival of his brother or sister. The anticipation continues to grow.

She put her novel down for a moment. What will he or she be like? What will he or she achieve? What kind of career will he or she have? Will he or she marry and have children? These musings would come to reality one way or another soon enough.

Two weeks before the due date, with things-in-motion and contractions established, they presented themselves to Frimley Park Hospital for another routine appointment.

And there it stopped.

Or rather 'they' stopped…the contractions, some short time after initial examination and assessment in the hospital. The option was offered for them to stay until labour was re-established or go home in the interim. Home was not far away and, decision made, it was to be a further two weeks before they returned to the hospital.

Generally, but not exclusively, second confinements tend to be shorter than the first. This one, however, was to be some eighteen and a half hours long, beating the former by two hours. During this time she was denied anything to eat or drink and could only ingest the aroma of the numerous cups of coffee thoughtfully provided for him by one of the nurses.

He had brought along some tapes of The Navy Lark and Round the Horne (remember cassettes?). Great entertainment though they were, having repeated the episodes many times that night they were word-perfect by the morning and more in a state of Round the Bend.

Number #2 son (baby Christopher) arrived with somewhat of a rush at exactly midday on 27th August 1992. The charge nurse offered 11:59 a.m. but was over-ruled by the senior midwife (Monica, if memory serves correctly), who had taken charge of the delivery and established 12:00 as the precise time of birth.

This meant that there would of necessity be another twenty-four hours in the hospital before mother and baby were to be allowed home. Baby had appeared to be rather mottled at birth but noisy nonetheless.

After being hosed down he was gratefully received into the care of his mother. Their joy and contentment was no less than that of the first delivery. The two doctors who had been summoned for reasons not actually outlined at the time, arrived in haste just after the birth and retired in similar fashion shortly afterwards.

In hindsight the extra time in the hospital acted as welcome rest and recuperation and, of course, allowed the hospital to monitor any consequential developments. The senior midwife was very experienced and it is possibly not without good reason that the extra period of baby monitoring was available.

Her parents arrived to visit and, in view of the distance travelled, had obviously dropped everything to be at their daughter's side as soon as they could.

Coming an altogether shorter distance was Thomas, who had been kept up to speed with developments during the pregnancy and was now about to see what all the fuss had been about. He did not say too much this first time but was obviously pleased to see Mum again, content and relaxed in bed. He then made his way round to the side of the bed where baby Christopher was wrapped up nice and warm in an open-topped clear plastic crib known as a 'fish tank'.

He raised himself on tip-toe to peer over the top with quite the funniest reaction that could have been imagined; he just continued to peer…

"Hmmm," he may have thought. "So this is what it's all been about then?"

Far from any kind of conflict, however, both brothers love each other to distraction even today.

The now larger family left for home, their thanks fulsome to all who had been involved during their time at the hospital.

Home already accommodated separate siblings who were as yet unaware of the new addition to the family. They were themselves brother and sister; Dandelion and Burdock. Dandelion was a large, flexible, passive black and white male cat who, apart from occasionally stretching up to see what was in the cot just standing there as a new piece of furniture, generally seemed to accept the newcomer with resigned approbation.

Burdock was the smaller of the two, being a white-bibbed tortoiseshell cat who took an altogether greater interest in this newcomer.

Burdock, positively and most unexpectedly, entered into a protective motherly phase and was many times seen to settle down very close to baby Christopher, in what could only be described as a maternal manner. She would frequently and notably take guard beneath his cot when he was in it, wherever it was in the house. Animals are smart in ways which even now are not fully recognised or understood. There is a separate train of thought that cats are autistic…who knows?

Christopher was a lovely, very happy, rather placid, affectionate, cuddly, quiet young baby. A second son who had a comprehensive appetite, eating and drinking almost anything put in front of him as long as he had a toy to play with at the time. Then overnight he stopped eating. He just stopped eating – **overnight!**

A change of travel arrangements

When planning a holiday the idea is to cover all necessary arrangements and eventualities before setting off. Think itinerary, tickets, passports, travel plans, clothes, toiletries, money, camera, suntan cream (hopefully), towels, maps, books, and more. The holiday destination would have been planned a long time ago. The anticipation and excitement for the impending journey continues to grow.

Having a child is rather like planning to go on holiday and generally, once in transit, the way is set fair for the destination. However, what if you don't actually get to your planned destination? Perhaps the destination was to be Paris but you, as a mother, find yourself in Amsterdam.

How the heck did that happen? Something is not right here.

CHAPTER THREE

Your Child Is Autistic – Go And Have A Nice Life

The MMR Injection:	*23rd November 1993.*
Chris's Referral:	*Children's Clinic (Early Summer 1995, not yet three years old.)*

It was quite true. One day in 1995 Chris drank his milk as usual and then arbitrarily refused his food – any food – all food, point blank. To this day the reason why remains unresolved. He was coaxed and cajoled into trying to eat anything at all. Milk would only be taken from a baby bottle with a teat. Then – a breakthrough. Tomato soup from Mum's spoon.

There was some very, very, slow progress for weeks on end with bananas crushed in milk as the only food he would eat. Then came bananas mashed up with Rice Krispies – a dubious concoction which, if not consumed within ten minutes of preparation, would set in the bowl like black concrete. Then plain white bread. Then bread and butter. Then bread and butter with thin chicken or turkey slices. All this over an extended period and with the very best of gentle persuasion.

Mum vividly recalls the time when Chris was two and a half years of age and she was trying to get him to say "please" for his drink. He declined to do so and walked away – here evidently he

An Autistic Sun

Christopher's University Challenge

Not a book about autism

A book about a boy who just happens to be autistic

Find us on **f**   "Mike Thorpe and an autist"

had understood the request either verbally or by reason of body language, but by walking away he did not get his drink until much later. Another lesson learnt. Fluids were otherwise usually not problematic. His food experiences were to expand incrementally, but very slowly, as time went on.

Alarm bells began to sound, not only in terms of the food situation but other aspects of his demeanour were of increasing concern.

Things were noticeably different this time around, measured against the relatively precocious development of Thomas. Chris was rather too placid, wouldn't or couldn't talk, wouldn't or couldn't walk. Detailed attention was evidently called for here by his mother in terms of his overall development, or lack of it. It was irrefutable that the professionals needed to be consulted, and as a matter of some urgency. A call to the Health Visitor resulted in a referral of mother and child to a doctor specialising in paediatric assessments. This did not go well.

All this was a terrible day-to-day load and strain to be carried by Mum. She had so much to cope with, being effectively on her own in terms of support and having to accommodate Thomas in his early school days into the bargain. Dad was temporarily out of the country at the time, working in Paris from Monday to Friday, so she had to bear the brunt in the interim.

She had no family to call on within an eighty mile radius and later admitted that at the time she had felt very alone, helpless and vulnerable. Not a good place to be. Who could she turn to? Who could she speak to? What help, if any, was available – and from where? The weekends could not come soon enough.

Diagnosis…

The diagnosis of autism was given at the referral appointment. The paediatrician delivered this serious news in what, it has to be said, was perceived to be a most off-hand and detached manner.

She was told by the doctor:

"He's on the autistic spectrum. No, it's nothing to do with your age. No, it's nothing to do with what you have or have not done. It just means he will need extra help with his education."

And that was **it**!

No information sheet. No facts and figures. No prognosis. No reference to any publications, clubs, associations, leaflets or other supporting literature of any kind. This was well before the advent and benefit of the internet.

A situation of stunning insensitivity by the standards of today. In effect:

"Go away and have a nice life."

Mum was absolutely distraught at the time and missing her husband more than could be imagined. He should have been there with her.

Two weeks later the Health Visitor rang to ask how she got on.

"Oh well," was her reaction. "At least you know now."

Nothing more than that...for years! Not very constructive input at such a sensitive and needy time.

Dad arrived back home from the continent on the Friday to hear the news for the first time, since she had decided to keep it to herself until he got home. This was not a good time by any stretch of the imagination, and it was clear that family life would follow a different path in future in terms of outlook and plans. After the distress on that particular day, it was then a matter of considering a rather large question.

"Where do we go from here then?"

Now was not the time to get angry. Now it was time to see what could be done.

The anticipated metaphorical trip to Paris may well have ended up in Amsterdam and having a child with a disability was going to be challenging – no doubt about that. Mum claimed there was nothing actually wrong with this because it was merely a different destination. She was in Amsterdam and quite content to be so, with the love and support of her husband and Thomas. She would only move on from there as and when the future dictated, and provided it would be in the company of those she loved.

The impact of friends and friendships was to become a great boon to her in so many ways in the future. Friends she already had, and many of those she did not yet have knowledge of, would become well-established, close, life-long friends.

Parental musings

Chris was as happy as any child to be wheeled around in his buggy on expeditions from home. Going from one to the other of adjacent Tesco and M&S superstores in Sandhurst would, however, induce a reaction to the extent that he would immediately become upset when going into the M&S store. This often happened as soon as the entrance to M&S was breached and he would quickly cover his ears as much as he could. This should not be taken to represent sympathy with the state of Dad's credit card balance. Contact with some other stores gave a similar reaction, notably in Toys R Us, where he would sometimes have to be taken out of the store so he could readjust in his own good time.

The conclusion drawn at the time was that there might have been something in the noise or frequency of the lighting that caused that reaction. It was already known that Chris had the most acute sense of hearing. Sudden other noises such as thuds, bangs and exploding balloons also caused him discomfort, as would being in close proximity to the somewhat higher pitch output of crying babies.

Later research confirmed that exposure to certain flickering neon lights could indeed elicit a classic autistic reaction by way of discomfort from the nature of the frequencies involved.

It may have been that his reactions came from more than one source, be it noise, fluorescent lighting, heat, smell or some other feature, in effect giving information overload to all those delicate preceptors he was poking out into the world. He would deliberately take new things into his possession and smell them. Thinking back it would have been impossible in the early days for the family to have any inkling of the impact of all those new smells he had been exposed to. Surely all his senses would have been vulnerable.

In relation to the wider context of noise, there was evident concern where Chris might be exposed to several separate or competing noises. This, he was later able to agree, was due to the fact that he had no way to filter out noises he did not need to hear or which had no relevance to him.

He was effectively listening to each conversation or noise within his compass. A measure of sensory overload from his perspective would be quite understandable. Combining this with his acute sense of hearing led to times when he would appreciate occasionally wearing headphones. He has now developed much more filter control.

Unless he was addressed directly by his own name when he was wanted, or he was to be given a request or an action, he would effectively ignore any such verbal contact, thinking that amongst all the other audio signals he was getting, this did not directly apply to him. A particular example of this came later at school when on occasion information handouts were left on the side for collection by all at the end of the class. Until he learnt better, Chris would not have picked one up as a matter of course unless specifically requested by name to do so.

It was not that he was a disobedient child, far from it, but one of the ways his parents learnt to get Chris's attention, and to improve on his 'filtering', was always to specifically mention his name when any verbal contact was to be directed at him. This soon became accepted practice and worked very well within the family, indeed so well that it extends by default to the present day. In practice, he understands the impact and probable consequences of almost anything said to him now as a matter of course.

Chris reacted when he was having his hair cut in the early days. Not violently so but the procedure was evidently uncomfortable for him. It seemed his hair was rather more sensitive than his scalp.

On a separate occasion, before he had learnt to walk, he was scuttling very fast along the lounge carpet on his hands and knees, back and forth, back and forth as he was wont to do. He missed a back and forth and rammed his head into one of the doors of the mahogany sideboard so hard that he actually broke it in.

The sharp intake of parental breath may be imagined here, in anticipation of the expansive roar of pain and understandable show of histrionics from Chris. Not so...there was a further short time lapse whilst he rubbed his head where it had struck and promptly set off again in the other direction, back and forth as before without even a whimper. Interesting behaviour indeed. Why should his hair appear to be so sensitive yet his cranium apparently not so? A conundrum.

This patrolling activity was a common characteristic of his behaviour even after he learnt to walk. Walking was something he achieved in his own time with great satisfaction to himself and the rest of the family, but the interesting behaviour continued. It seemed that learning to walk and talk were, in some respects, achieved rather late in his development but it was thought not dramatically so at the time. Hindsight is a wonderful thing.

There is no intention to infer or assign responsibility or blame here, but there was a change in Chris after he had the MMR (Measles, Mumps and Rubella) injection in November 1993.

There were other attributes such as fluttering actions with his arms and occasional guttural gurgling sounds from his throat. In terms of his general behaviour, apart from the previously noted reactions to noise and sensory overload situations, he had every right to be regarded as being a well-behaved young lad. He was not liable to lash out or be disruptive. Really he was no bother at all.

Memories have been racked to try and recall if there were any evident signs that Chris was different in any way prior to the MMR jab. Nothing springs to mind as there was no reason or driver at the time to focus on any possible autistic attributes.

Whether the injection was or was not the precise cause of any change in Chris, or just a contributing factor, or just an unfortunate result of rare statistical probability related to such a change is an open question debated even to this day. The family wrote a thirteen-page letter to the doctor's practice with regard to Chris's situation, which resulted in minimal satisfaction and resolution.

The intention here is to put such pointed musings to one side in terms of the content of this book because nothing would have changed the circumstances the family had to cope with. Their philosophy was that, although many others could well be in a worse situation, this did not make things any easier when coping with Chris's needs.

Consider...

You may or may not be directly associated with someone who is on the autistic spectrum. Consequently, the intention here is not to get too involved with the science of the condition but bring the following particular observations to the fore.

Interest may be from the point of view of actually raising an autistic child, the impact of late diagnosis of autism, the approach of a professional in the field, concerned supporter or just human interest. You may indeed be autistic yourself.

The broad range of the condition of autism may make some of the following observations appear rather general in nature. They do, however, bear consideration.

- Autism is notoriously difficult to diagnose.

- On BBC Breakfast TV for 26th April 2017, there was a feature about a young lad from Wales with autism, which was to be broadcast on 2nd May 2017. The presenter, Charlie Stayt, opened the segment with the observation that it was reported some 700,000 people in the UK suffered from some form of autism ...go figure.

- Having earlier said that there was no intention of getting too involved with the science, the following definition, one of many in the public domain, is offered.

  "Autism spectrum disorder (ASD) – a neurological development disorder – is a disability that is caused by differences in how the brain functions. People with ASD may communicate, interact, behave, and learn in different ways."

- Diagnosis is rare at ages rather less than three years old. With the greater awareness available today, it is not at all uncommon to hear in the media of someone being diagnosed as autistic while being well into middle age.

- The whole subject of autism is getting more and more exposure to the world at large. This is no bad thing at all. The need for continued development of assistance, care, concern and understanding remains.

- The consequences of autism are more easily identified than the reasons for it.

- Autism is a life-long condition.

- Autism is not curable in the accepted sense of the word but the consequences and impacts can be influenced by personal development, external interactive support and management.

- Some autists may demonstrate significant development capabilities whilst growing up, particularly if they have some initial basis of cognitive development to draw on in their own way.

- The condition of autism was separately and specifically recognised, or classified, in the USA, circa 1945. Before that time, autists would have been lumped together with a whole range of others with 'special needs'. Each with their own particular developmental, physiological, neurological and psychological attributes and characteristics. Not a very constructive state of affairs. Since 1945 great steps have been made regarding the nature and treatment of this very wide subject. Thank goodness for the progress being made of late.

- Autism is commonly described as the 'invisible disability' since external appearance often gives no insight or identification of such a condition, or in many cases, of any apparent disability whatsoever.

- At the time Chris was diagnosed in 1995, there was

no internet to speak of to be able to research the condition.

- The autistic spectrum is incredibly wide, encompassing a whole range of abilities and personal attributes differing with each individual.

- Autists do not naturally seek or need the sort of social interaction that non-autists find necessary and enjoyable.

- Asperger's syndrome is a form of autism but generally accepted as a distinctly separate, though complementary, condition.

- Chris might be described as being a high-functioning autist in the language of those professionals concerned with the analysis of the disability. He is not, however, Asperger's and does very much empathise with how people feel and he would be the first to be concerned if someone was in evident distress, either physically or emotionally.

- Whether someone is actually capable of being made to be autistic is an unrealistic concept to pursue.

- The earlier work of Dr Andrew Wakefield in the field of autism is now largely discredited.

- Research has been undertaken regarding the nature of certain preservative agents, such as thimerosal, used in childhood vaccines. Thimerosal is a mercury-based preservative used for decades in the USA in multi-dose vials of medicines and vaccines although, according to reports, not used in MMR vaccines in the USA. In any event, the use of it has relatively recently been discontinued in all childhood vaccines. Aluminium is found in some vaccines and although lead may be found in water, it is reasonable to expect that this is excluded from vaccines these days.

- In the UK there has been a marked reluctance on the part of the authorities to consider the MMR vaccine being given as three separate injections.

- Males are more likely to be autistic than females. There is ample research available regarding 'x' and 'y' chromosomes, but it would appear to be simplistic to say that it is all down to the 'y' one. This would then indicate that only males could be autistic and this is far from the case in practice.

- In the 1990s, research indicated that as many as 10% of the new-born in Surrey could be on the autistic spectrum.

- In the early 1990s, the county of Surrey was considered to have a significantly greater provision for meeting the needs of those on the autistic spectrum than neighbouring counties.

- Autists have a range of talents and abilities sometimes markedly greater than those of their peers, but evident in different and sometimes highly focussed ways. This might mark them out as being thought of as unusual, different or even threatening due to that very difference.

- People with severe autism commonly have little or no speech and may sometimes be construed as tending to have a violent disposition. If that is the case, surely any such tendency would primarily be as a consequence of utter frustration with the inability to make themselves understood or to be able to communicate properly?

- Autists generally appreciate, and will usually respond favourably to, a fixed or regular timetable or schedule of events. Having learnt such systems, they find this a way of controlling their own day.

- Repetitive actions are often a feature of autistic behaviour. Any imposed modification to established behaviour patterns may cause an upset until the modified behaviour pattern is learnt, understood and accepted. Those with more severe autism may find such disruption harder to come to terms with.

- Autists are creatures of habit and can be upset by surprises or disturbances to a routine.

- Chris likes routine and has a wonderful singing voice. In spite of several attempts to progress this vocal development by suggesting he join a choir, he has always resisted. His argument is that having sung a song once, he knows it – why should he have to practise and practise? This is another example of why autists are not normally 'team players'.

- When an autist makes progress or exhibits a measurable improvement either in or out of school, this almost invariably remains in place. At school this is why so many of the helpers, teachers and teaching assistants find autistic progress so rewarding. It represents the knowledge that they themselves have been able to deliver and make a difference.

- Based on personal experience with Chris, one way to approach dealing with autism is not by being unfailingly and unrealistically optimistic but by applying cautious, dedicated, constructive intent.

- What drugs or herbal treatments might be appropriate, applicable, or useful? Parental research of this sensitive area at the time led to the conclusion that nothing was actually going to change Chris. It was considered necessary to avoid all sorts of snake oil remedies. They settled on a regular course of multivitamins and minerals plus a daily Omega 3 fish oil capsule for him.

- There is no escaping the fact that there are many challenges in bringing up autistic children, particularly as no two autists are the same.

- If every minute of every day is spent trying to analyse and explain autism in terms of 'analyst speak', then this will be with the loss of experiencing fulfilling, life-affirming attributes given, received and returned.

CHAPTER FOUR

What's With All The Flapping?

The early years

Assimilation, development and assessments were now the order of the day.

Mum was to give up work during her pregnancies, but what about afterwards? Would she then give up work completely to care for the two boys? Yes, of course.

In 1995, Chris was diagnosed as having speech and communication difficulties on the autistic spectrum. Aspects of his diagnosis meant he would need considerable support throughout his education and beyond.

Some details of his particular case are worthy of note.

- There are those who might consider that a diagnosis of autism infers the subject is no longer a sentient being. Others might consider it is no more of a disability than a severe head cold. Both are outrageous exaggerations and not what the family ascribes to.

- Dad and Mum are averse to the constant attempts of others to categorise people both generally and specifically, but accept that in Chris's case the importance of his diagnosis is an entirely different matter. He is, in effect, pigeon-holed for life.

- Chris's diagnosis of autism is indisputably appropriate and puts his progress on a different path to that of most neuro-typicals (i.e. the rest of us).

- There was no significant information on the subject of autism available to the family in the early days. No easily accessible manual and no evident general assistance or interactive help.

- The family did not have the assistance of an assigned Social Worker and support from the Health Worker was effectively non-existent.

- It was only by chance that Mum heard about the DLA (Disability Living Allowance) from another mother at Thomas's primary school. This is a legitimate entitlement for Chris. The lengthy benefits form was duly sourced, completed and submitted with the majority of the content not relevant to autism. Happily the DLA benefit was subsequently secured.

- Sheltered housing accommodation provision for Chris is currently not an option.

- Provision of a parental Motability disability motor car is not an option.

- A Blue Badge disability sticker for the family car is not an option.

- Discounted theatre and cinema tickets are available for Chris and one accompanying carer.

- Increased writing time during exams is provided.

- Discounted travel concessions are available by virtue of his disability.

- A measure of heightened awareness by school staff and medical practitioners is necessary by virtue of his diagnosis.

- He is unlikely ever to own or drive a car although he would be well capable of learning to drive and possibly passing the driving test.

- It is improbable, though not impossible, that he will ever marry or have children.

Mum would be the one to spend most time with Chris during the working week. When Dad got back home, there were always questions asked as to how things had been during the day.

How would anyone know if Chris had any health concerns over and above the eminently visible drippy doze (nose)? When a child has autism, a mother's protection, dedication, care and attention stretches over a longer time frame and to a more acute degree than for children without such a disability. Interpretation of body language and, in Chris's case, him not necessarily being able to verbalise what he might think was wrong with him, were ever-present concerns in earlier times. In time Chris's improved ability to be more interactive here increased to the extent that now he has a fairly fully established self-diagnosis system.

In earlier days he would listen in on family conversations and respond naturally enough when bidden, but he was not the most communicative, nor would he usually be the first to initiate a conversation. It was quite apparent, however, that he understood most of what was being talked about.

He would go to some lengths to avoid eye to eye contact and had the habit of turning his head to one side, looking out of one side of the corner of his eye. This used to be quite disconcerting and it was important to resist the temptation to walk over to him, take his head in both hands and force him not to look away. That would have been a very bad thing to do on so many levels.

When young, his corneas were dilated and, if he would be still for long enough so that one could look into his eyes, they were like black empty pools drawing one in. Now those eyes are lovely colours of light, life, laughter and knowledge. Now when you look him straight in the eye, he smiles. How's that for neurological development?

The question "Why?" applies to almost any matter regarding Chris, his condition and his progress. Such questions require resolution or dismissal. These concerns have generally been replaced with a "Wow, look at him now, he can do...!"

With no extended family on hand and with those family members who might have been available, still alive or further flung than conveniently able to offer assistance, Dad and Mum went their own way, just getting on with things. Contact was maintained with the doctor's surgery.

Chris would quite often say "no" when asked if he would like to try something new in the way of food. Clearly this was his own internal defence mechanism because he really had a chicken-and-egg or catch-22 situation as far as food was concerned. He would not try something unless he knew he liked it, yet was particularly reticent in the early days even to try something new, in spite of how appetisingly it might have been presented. This was where very gentle encouragement and persuasion came in.

Chris would need to learn everything for himself before he knew he wanted to do it. An easy statement to make but, as an instance, he was seven years old before he actually sucked through a straw, yet as a baby, there was never any reluctance to take the conventional bottle of milk. Many ways had been tried to get this mechanism over to him and one day it just clicked. Rather than blowing nice bubbles he should simply suck.

Getting him to blow his nose when necessary was an entirely separate challenge requiring an investment in copious amounts of Kleenex tissues. (Note from Dad – other brands of tissues are also available.)

Chris had trouble translating what he was being asked to do, into actually completing even the simplest of tasks. He could be shown how to do something, but it would not be until he had actually done it himself that the penny would drop. He would then know to answer yes or no for that particular matter in the future.

He has always had a thirst for knowledge with a mind committed to learning and understanding. Even today he has a fervent desire for facts and figures and has developed this into a measure of demonstrating independent imagination. A great step forward in his progress. He would always read books, encyclopaedia or manuals for facts, but now might well also select a work of fiction, based on one of his many games interests or pastimes.

The health practice community nurse did come round to see the family when Chris was quite young but frankly was found not to be of any particular or constructive help in terms of Chris's condition or perceived needs. She considered the family to be in denial. This was a point of view not at all consistent with the approach the family wished their hopes for the future to be based upon.

No overt criticism is implied here but the family soldiered on …and on.

A matter of black and white

Those of a mature age who regard delving into a sturdy book as a suitable substitute for strenuous exercise probably remember black and white television. This is all there used to be, well until the national anthem played and the little white spot eventually disappeared. The images were actually more akin to dark grey versus lighter grey on the screen and in the early days of soap powder adverts, the white shirts were actually yellow in the film studio in order to increase the contrast when broadcast.

Dad is of the opinion that most of the Second World War was actually fought out in black and white, there being so relatively little by way of a colour record of the events.

For years there has been an interest in machines designed to achieve the nirvana of flight powered solely by direct human effort, and many early black and white film clips exist showing commitment to that end.

There used to be an annual competition where suitably mad contestants (sorry – wannabe pilots) would throw themselves off a seaside pier complete with their craft, only to reach the salty stuff below somewhat earlier than intended. (The advent of colour broadcasting merely served to make this a more enjoyably scatty visual treat for the viewers.)

A classic example of black and white television showed someone who had spent more time than he should have attempting to make what can only be described as a flying-bedstead. This, contrary to some previous examples, actually had a form of reciprocating engine on board in an attempt to drive the wings up and down with rapid motion and thereby achieve flight.

Sad to say the actual end was rather less elegant and resulted in a total failure of the whole enterprise, with bed-knobs and broomsticks flung to all corners amid the de-constructed machine.

Chris used to flap his hands in a similar manner – happily without the same end result.

Discussions...discussions...

In the early days Chris exhibited some unexpected and different characteristics from what might have been regarded as the norm. Parental concern and curiosity as to the reasons why this should be needed to be investigated to try to rationalise the differing aspects of autism evident in his make-up. There were many points to consider and these were by no means common to all autists in the way that influenza or migraine might be to the wider world. Autists demonstrate a wide range of variables and no two autists are the same. The immediate concern was to relate these features to Chris's situation.

Having started on this journey of enlightenment...

Many kids with autism flap their hands. There are two observations to be made here. The first is that nobody really knows why. The second is that many people think they know why, having spent many detailed hours of study presenting ever more involved descriptions and purported scientific analyses, primarily in order to promote their own self-interest in publishing papers, satisfying medical exams or medical institution advancement criteria. A lot of this jargon has very little value to the man or woman on the street, especially those at the coal-face.

Being a family at the coal-face, there is the fervent hope that, at some stage in the future, the increasing amount of research and analysis in support of the subject of autism will result in concrete progress rather than just a continued exchange of opinions.

There is no cure as such for autism, so there is the continuing need for a balanced, in-depth, observational treatment of the subject, combined with detailed development paths to assist autists. Surely this is a valid approach representing a positive contribution to their lives.

Dad is here reminded of a thermodynamics lecture way back in 1964 at what was originally Woolwich Polytechnic (then to be Thames Polytechnic and now the University of Greenwich). Here, apart from entreating his students to read *Brighter Than A Thousand Suns* by Robert Jungk (a book about the history of atomic scientists), the lecturer waxed lyrical on matters of heat and temperature. His proposition in terms of temperature was that nobody at that time had yet come up with an adequate definition of the term.

Many could describe what it actually represented, and what the consequences of it were, but as far as a pure definition for temperature was concerned, the jury was still out. The implied link here between what Chris is, what he says and what he does, represents grounds for further research. It could take quite some time.

Characteristics...

So if the definition of autism is a matter of much discussion, it is easier back at the coal-face to comment on certain autistic characteristics and try to make progress that way.

There has been a deliberate attempt to avoid packing out this book with multiple downloads from the internet, primarily because it would serve no benefit, not suit the premise of the book and no exhaustive study of them has been made by the parents anyway. Life is just too short. Remember this is not a book about autism but about a boy who just happens to be autistic.

There are some non-attributable internet references outlined here, however, by way of observation and response from a Seattle-based website, along with some of Dad's comments.

Observation:

Children with autism tend to have repetitive motor behaviour characteristics such as waving or flapping of hands. These arm and hand motions may be accompanied by other motor mannerisms such as jumping or head turning.

Response #1:

Repetitive motor mannerisms such as flapping hands, tensing parts of the body, jumping or dancing, are often linked to strong emotions such as excitement or frustration. We see similar behaviour in babies who eventually grow out of this behaviour.

Response #2:

These may also be self-soothing aspects and/or attempts at self-regulation when what is perceived as overwhelming upset, excitement, boredom or anxiety are present.

Dad comment #1:

"Could write a book on these points alone."
This represents classic **Chris** responses which were in evidence during a large period of his youth. Again, the point here should be to explain, to reason, to develop, not to leave an observation as just an observation. It must be said that the sight of a baby jumping or dancing presumably before the onset of the ability to achieve vertical status is an interesting concept.

Dad comment #2:

"Head turning has disappeared from **Chris**'s lexicon."
Jumping and dancing are less evident in him, though when the

family is out together, he will occasionally still exhibit a small skip in his step as an involuntary, inconsequential, isolated twitch. The hand flapping has subsided from extensive semaphore to occasional twiddling of the fingers, drumming or drawing fingers up his thigh in the form of a frantic short-term itch when noticeably excited or pleased. Freemantles school would have had some influence in the modification and morphing of this attribute.

Dad comment #3:

"The evidence of Chris's reactions being linked to emotion or excitement is clear and conclusive."

There is no doubt about that at all. In terms of Response #2 above though, how can a very young baby invoke self-regulation or self-control over overwhelming upset, excitement, boredom or anxiety? This surely implies a neurological development and control out of kilter with the extremely immature nature of the subject. What babies do when they need attention is to make a noise.

If such differential responses from those who may go on to have a confirmed diagnosis of autism are so different from the norm and they could be controlled by self-regulation, why aren't all babies and little ones capable of consistent behaviour? This may well be one of the appropriate markers in the diagnosis of autism by those in white coats. Remember, autism is notoriously difficult to diagnose and conventionally, diagnosis is linked to perceived developmental progress when the subject is generally about three years old.

Dad comment #4:

"Overwhelming fear, emotion, frustration and excitement are matters of deep concern and worthy of prolonged consideration."

Dad Comment #5:

"Chris is still inclined to pace up and down in his room."

This is seen as an intermittent, distracted process, largely on the basis of habit and evident only when he is concentrating on a specific aspect of one of his games or possibly musing on the general instability of the cosmos.

Here we go again…

"Many kids with autism walk on their toes."

Observation:

Toe-walking may be a learned habit because many toddlers walk on their toes or it may relate to motor coordination challenges, a tight Achilles tendon, or a sensory processing difference. Toe-walking is also seen with other neurological or developmental disorders, such as cerebral palsy.

Response #1:

Children with autism often present with stereotypical motor movements, one of which may be walking on tip-toe. Others hypothesize that walking on tip-toe reduces over-stimulation in the feet that can occur as a result of walking on the entire foot.

Dad comment:

"Yes, Chris is still inclined to do this."

Wearing boots or shoes when outdoors, of course, masks this feature somewhat. It has been an effort to get him to walk consistently from heel to toe. When out and about, he will also tend to scuff his heels because he forgets to walk properly. Suggestions for him to lift his knees when he walks are only

37

occasionally successful. When in bare feet at home he regularly walks on the balls of his feet. He knows he does it but has not yet successfully explained why.

For the third and last time here...

"Many kids with autism avoid eye contact."

Observation:

There is a difference between kids who actively avoid eye contact and kids who haven't learned how to use eye contact during communication. For active avoiders there appears to be a sensory component where it is unpleasant for them to make direct eye to eye contact.

Response #1:

One of the core deficits for individuals with autism is difficulty coordinating verbal and non-verbal means of communication. For example, while speaking to someone, a child may forget to make eye contact. This makes it difficult to know to whom the verbalization is directed. In addition, individuals with autism do not find satisfactory communicative meaning in others' eyes like the rest of us. Thus, they are not drawn to others' eyes as information sources.

Response #2:

...because of difficulty attaching meaning to the facial cues of caregivers and peers which relate to the child's social-communication skills.

Dad comment:

"A most evident characteristic of Chris's life which became markedly less noticeable as school became a necessary part of his development."

With trust and good grace he will now keep still long enough to allow Dad or Mum to look deep into his eyes and see the myriad of colours on display. These were simply not there earlier.

Decisions...decisions...

With the decision having been made for Mum to stop working for a living, there was another important, though non-fiscal matter to consider. With her described as an elderly (but still very nice) primigravida in terms of Thomas, the family was now in receipt of two children. A bonus by any standard but Dad had already determined that there should be no further attempt to engage the country average number of children per family of 2.4 as a target. He was unsure what could be done with 0.4 of a child and preferred integers anyway. So the home discussion was brief and non-contentious.

The only question then was how to proceed. Garden shears were regarded as an altogether unacceptable option. The two half brick method was discounted on the basis that it could hurt if one got one's thumbs in the way. So back to Frimley Park Hospital it was. She remained in the reception area, talking to the receptionist in front of a row of nervous men regarding the matter in hand, to be greeted by her husband on his return from the procedure holding on to the door frame as if for dear life.

Said he to the surgeon...

"How long afterwards can I, can we, well...you know what I mean?"

Came the response...

"I suggest you wait until you get home."

That is the absolute truth. Scout's honour.

CHAPTER FIVE

What About Those Numbers?

Playing on his own when young, Chris developed the habit of manipulating the alphabet letters on the several sets he had been given as toys. He appeared fascinated by, and concerned with, concentrating on the numbers on the number blocks and individual number tablets as if trying to make some sense of them. This interest in numbers continues to the present day but in different and less overt ways.

Another feature which was a great boon at this time was the advent of VHS video tapes (remember them?). Nursery tales, rhymes, children's stories and the like could now be lifted from the written page, re-imaged, shared and enjoyed at any time. There was the legendary "I'm a little tea pot short and stout, here's my handle, here's my spout", "Bananas in Pyjamas" and so many more. When the video player was not in action, the television was quite often on at home anyway on one channel or another.

Not so long after Chris had started to talk, something rather remarkable happened in relation to the TV programme, *Countdown*, with the ticking clock and the urbane Richard Whitely in charge, supported by the lively Carol Vorderman. Chris was nestled down with Mum in the armchair.

For the numbers round, Carol picked up the allotted selection of blocks and placed them in turn in the slots with the numbers clearly shown on the screen. Instantly, and it has to be understood this really was that quick, Chris said a number.

"Huhh?" questioned Dad.

What Chris had done was to add up each of the numbers to give a grand total. It was double-checked and found to be correct.

"How? Why?"

Well, that happened each time Carol laid up a series of numbers. Chris did not yet have the ability to use those numbers to calculate the target number (that being the next activity in the programme), nevertheless this was thought to be nothing short of astonishing.

The television was turned off.

"Chris, said Dad, what is two plus two?"

"Four!" came the response and instantly.

"Chris, what is four plus four?"

"Eight."

"What is eight plus…?"

The answers continued just as quickly into the thousands. The parents were blown away – this was something really special.

In between those ears evidently lurked an embryonic mathematical mind.

From these beginnings, Chris was consistently able to demonstrate a truly lightning ability to mentally add and subtract correctly, almost without fail. That he possesses a phenomenal and photographic memory might lead to the view that this helped with these sums, but here the point is that this would simply be in the mechanism of the calculation. Whilst it may be useful to remember how to execute individual sums, a photographic memory can only be of minor assistance as different sums involve manipulating different numbers.

A large degree of credit should go to the cassette of the times-tables played to exhaustion in the car. Despite the random points of access to the tape whenever Chris was in the car, somehow he assimilated the entire set of times tables in a chronological and coherent way. Chris's schooling started basic numeracy leading to hard-sums with pencil and paper before ultimately progressing to the calculator. Such a grounded way of learning is invaluable for any child.

Multiplication and long division took slightly longer to master. It seemed no time at all, however, before not only was he using a hand held calculator at school but, as with everyone else, was free to take it into almost any exam room. Dad, he of the slide-rule-and-book-of-log-tables generation, found this new-found liberalism intriguing to say the least.

Although competent with the functionality of his calculator, Chris persisted with his same way of doing things and would only do the calculation once. Being shown how, and with what purpose, particular buttons operated was not the whole story here because Chris thought every calculation he did was correct the first time he did it – not necessarily so.

A common adage in calculator usage is 'rubbish in – rubbish out'. Even at the manipulation stage of his calculations Chris had to be taught to slow down and make sure his input was valid. This helped towards achieving consistently correct answers.

In engineering industries where numbers can be quite large, the real issue is to get some form of satisfaction that the sums are actually correct, based on the figures put into the calculation in the first place. Conventionally, the best way to do this is to repeat the calculation as a cross-check. Hence the second adage, 'measure twice – cut once'.

With much patience and practice it did come to be an automatic and worthwhile discipline for Chris to adopt the philosophy of calculating everything twice on a calculator. He was also exposed to the concept of "Does the answer look as though it is in the right sort of ball-park?" If it did, there was a chance that the computation had proved successful. His earlier experiences had resulted in that single calculation with no real appreciation of whether the answer was right or wrong. Now he would interrogate his actions to a greater degree the more he went on.

A parallel to be drawn here is in the Morecambe and Wise Show with Andre Previn as conductor, and Eric playing all the right notes but not necessarily in the right order.

CHAPTER SIX

Playing, Visiting & Thomas The Tank Engine

One of the things to enjoy with young children as a treat or when on holiday is to take them to the seaside.

Sandbanks beach is a very popular, gently sloping sandy beach just to the west of Bournemouth and the parents were used to going there as a couple. The party of four, now constituting the family, arrived bright and early on what was going to be a lovely sunny but busy day. The need for early arrival was to ensure a place in the pay-and-display car park right behind the beach.

The children were exhumed from the beach paraphernalia packed in the back of the car and the family progressed to the beach, collecting rented deck chairs on the way. Windbreaks were erected some ten feet away from the high water line, chairs established, towels and toys laid in place. Dad was assigned chief channel-in-the-sand-digger down to the water line, Mum assisted in the construction of the sturdy edifice of the sand castle by the expedient application of sundry flags leaving the heavy labour to others.

Chris had very good balance so it was no great surprise to see him standing erect on the sand, on his left leg, but licking the sole, repeat sole! of his right foot to clear it of this strange new material called sand. Interesting, clever, but no cigar.

The boys pottered whilst everyone waited upon the opening of the nearby beach kiosk which would produce the most wonderful tasting and cooked-while-you-looked hot, fresh, doughnut rings, much enhanced by the provision of a mug of tea. The day progressed and the beach filled.

Parental duties naturally require that young progeny are kept safe in such an environment and generally within view. Chris was, as ever, wont to walk to and fro, to and fro and, having the shoreline as a border, continued this activity at some length to and fro, to and...**Oops!**

"Sweetheart, where's Chris?!!?"

"Huhh? What? Where? When?"

"Ruddy 'ell!"

"I saw him just a moment ago!"

Swift action was the order of the day.

"Which way?"

Chris had progressed some 400 yards along the busy shore line by the simple expedient of failing to turn when perhaps he should have. Upon being apprehended he started to run back towards the family corral. Speedy blighter he was even then.

He made such good progress that before he reached his ultimate target he just sat down with a completely different family and started to play with their kids and their toys. Funniest thing seen all day. Chris was safely extracted after everyone had a good laugh and the day continued. Driving home, Dad mused on the events of the day with the other three fast asleep, worn out by the vagaries of the day and the surfeit of vitamin D. A good result.

To further illustrate Chris's innate sense of balance requires an additional variable in the guise of a large animate body of unpredictable disposition; a horse. Possible individual purchase and ongoing care of same fell well outside the family budget. Recommended by friends to expose him to the concept of horse riding, there was still the question as to how to achieve this. The family then had a 'light bulb' moment.

"How about Riding for the Disabled?"

Chris and his brother had experienced short duration horse rides at the annual Lightwater Church Summer Fayre. After initial apprehension, Chris appeared to take to it like a duck to water. From arrangements subsequently made through his school, he had the offer of three sessions of horse riding with others, under army tutelage in the care of the Brigadier's wife at the Sandhurst Military Academy, out in the open air. He enjoyed this very much, got on well, and was very comfortable doing it. He seemed a natural at horse riding.

After his three weeks' experience there, he went to a separate local establishment where riding took place under cover in an enclosed arena. The floor was covered with a mix of rubber blocks and sawdust. Much to everyone's regret, however, there was also a large mix of what may tastefully be described as a 'saline' atmosphere, based upon the entirely natural, but copious, liquid and solid discharges of the horses. Sadly Chris's eyes could not cope with the stringent impact and regrettably this form of recreation had to be abandoned.

Other trips…a selection

The journey to Waterloo by train and then on to North Greenwich underground station on the Jubilee Line was easy enough.

Question: Just where was the family going?

Answer: Somewhere rather interesting.

Having children is a fairly exceptional undertaking, on the basis of everything that goes with such packages. The script varies every time and the possibilities and variables are endless.

So, if children are thought only fairly exceptional, what, pray, can actually be considered truly exceptional?

Why not the Millennium Dome, nowadays re-badged as the O2? That was something definitely different and no mistake. There has been nothing like it before or since.

It was to be a truly substantial edifice and great interest followed all stages of the design, development and construction.

Do you choose not to go to visit it just because it cost a lot of money? It would, after all, be rather a long time to wait for the next Millennium.

The family decided they would visit it because it was fairly easy for them to do so and it would be of interest to see just what all the fuss had been about. They would then also be able to draw their own conclusions as to whether the concept was of value.

There is no intention here to cover the detail of the individual items, exhibits and events available at the time. Personal research will reveal the history regarding the nature of the wide range of options and features that were there.

Access on the day followed the short walk from North Greenwich tube station. The initial impact was "Wow – interesting!" There was a veritable feast for the eyes and senses. The content was varied with lots to see, lots to do, lots to interact with, lots to walk through and around, lots to provide food for thought. It was a good browse and just a completely different experience. It represented views of the future, current technology trends, as well as the more established order of things.

Chris's interest was stimulated. His eyes were everywhere and he took as much opportunity as he could to join in with the range of interactive features on offer.

It was interesting, informative, educational and indeed stimulating for the family. On balance…yes, it was a good place to have visited and pleasing to have consciously travelled there without preconceptions. Other people may demur but then that's life.

The family probably got more out of it than the lags involved in the planned, but failed, diamond heist raid there, which caused quite a stir in the media at the time. The attempted smash-and-grab had proved so tempting that the prospective thieves thought it worthwhile to pop along to test the security conditions in place rather than enrich their minds.

This visit to the Dome was made soon after it first opened. Two further family trips were undertaken, the third being on the very last day it was open. Just because the family could – just because they wanted to. A good day out each time.

Both boys had visited previously and independently with their respective schools, giving further opportunity for education in the broadest sense.

What the boys actually got out of the whole thing cannot be measured, although there would have been sufficient interest and stimulation. However, there is now, of course, no chance of a re-visit.

Further along

Trips to Legoland Windsor, Chessington World of Adventure near (err...Chessington) and Thorpe Park in Surrey were usually great fun and a good, though exhausting, family day out. At Legoland the family learnt that Chris would probably not drive a car later on in life.

There were two car circuits, one for little ones and a rather more formal one for those slightly older, where electrically operated cars were driven along the marked roadways, each driver utilising the stop and go pedals as necessary, together with control of the steering wheel. Each group of drivers was given a proper safety briefing before being allowed into the vehicles.

Thank goodness for that because, not long after the start, it was evident that some young 'erberts had only a nominal understanding of what they could and could not legitimately do on the road circuit. They approached adherence to the rules of the road with the same disdain sadly seen to this day on real roads by rather too many adult drivers.

Each time Chris visited the park and drove on that circuit, he obeyed all the rules of the road in accordance with the given instructions. This covered posture, traffic lights, lane discipline, overtaking, give way signs, stop signs; the whole caboodle. How could he, would he, be able to anticipate another driver's less than proper compliance with those same rules and regulations in real life?

Chris drove consistently but did not appear to be able to appreciate, or anticipate the possibility of mistakes, indolence, lack of concentration, or just plain bad driving on the part of other drivers. Happily at Legoland at least, there were to be no head-on collisions.

"Time for a pizza, Chris."

Getting lost is an occupational hazard when growing up. This action of displacement may continue into later life depending on circumstances and eventualities, but it naturally requires a certain level of management. Getting mislaid is a whole different ballgame and something generally restricted to those who are rather young and not yet sufficiently in control of their own mobility mechanisms...that is, unless a degree of autism is involved.

Experience shows that even with every care and attention given by parents or guardians, whenever there is a holiday, day trip, shopping trip or even just a visit to the local park, your friendly autist may become an elusive escapologist seemingly at a moment's notice. A simply mercurial ability.

Mum had mentally put away horror stories of children disappearing either deliberately or inadvertently in some of the larger theme parks. To start with she was nervous when it was just her and Chris out with friends and their own children. Chris would sometimes just walk off at Legoland. Once he was found some distance away having queued for a little train ride on a loop. He was happily going round and round, totally unconcerned and content, waving merrily. Having spied her prey, Mum approached the miscreant rapidly at the end of the ride. Another recapture was imminent.

On a separate occasion Chris was with Mum and big brother Thomas on a shopping trip to the superstores in Sandhurst. For a while he kept in close contact, walking alongside the shopping trolley, when there he was – gone in a flash. A small panic ensued. Mum stayed put at the till paying for the trolley full of shopping so Thomas was despatched on reconnaissance. Chris was subsequently located in the store next door, some way distant from the revolving doors at the entrance. Reconciliation meant the panic was resolved but, not for the first time, he was in receipt of a good talking to.

Chris was much later to say that he always knew where he was going at the time, which was some small comfort, but he was less able to vocalise why.

Several return visits were paid to the theme parks. One particularly fraught moment occurred on the Dragon Falls ride at Chessington World of Adventure, initially considered by the family to be just a leisurely water ride in individual family-sized boats. Mum was in the front of the boat with Thomas and Dad, with Chris snuggled on his shoulder, was on the bench seat behind. Nobody had realised just how high the boat had progressed until it reached the top of the ride.

With such rides, it will be appreciated that what goes up must come down. At the precise moment the boat began the rather eager descent by dint of gravity, Chris attempted to leap from Dad's shoulder and hightail it out of the back of the boat. Thank goodness, quick reactions saved the day, but this was just another example of how bringing up kids presents something of a challenge. (Check out the You Tube clip of the ride on the internet and sympathise...please!).

Whenever Dad sits down on a Saturday night to watch Match of the Day, Chris makes an appearance as if by magic to shout:

"Hello Jonathan Pearce!"

Accepting that this can be a distraction, especially if Dad is watching the Crystal Palace game, there is good reason for this. Chris became heavily involved in watching the original series of *Robot Wars* on the television and was really taken by the whole concept of the programme. Jonathon Pearce was the commentator for this as well as sometimes for Dad's football.

On one trip to Legoland in his early teenage years, there was a Robogedden featured display with actual TV show robots battling in an area reminiscent of a boxing ring. This was not just a display but an interactive performance, where Chris was able to take the controls of one of the modest-sized robots ('bots) from his corner of the ring and battle against three other opponents. Not only that, but he was multi-tasking by giving his broadcast impression of a Jonathon Pearce commentary over the loudspeaker, all with great aplomb. Recollection has it that he won his bout – why is that a surprise?

And then to Jersey...

The family went to Jersey in the Channel Islands for a holiday when Chris was eleven years old. Dad had been there before when he was at the same age but he still remembered things and places. Yes, the island was more modern now but everything seemed that much smaller. The weather was not nearly as nice as he remembered, but no matter, there was more than enough to see and do. Mum had also been to the island but way before knowing Dad. Towards the end of the week she said:

"Why don't we go to the Jersey Pottery?"

"Not so keen, but let's give it a go," said Dad, albeit with some reluctance.

Halfway through the visit there really did not seem to be much of interest happening and the kids were flagging. Dad was of a mind to meander...

Walking past a line of individual workstations where the inmates (sorry – staff!) were hand-painting individual pieces, all was quiet apart from the sound of a water feature in the background.

Some water feature this turned out to be! Dad turned round to see where Chris was and spied him instantly by the full length window in the corner, facing a large potted plant pot full of pebbles, with his kegs down around his ankles and unconcernedly, but deliberately, being the cause of the water feature.

The sight of Chris's moony will be forever etched on Dad's consciousness.

"Oh my word!"

Speedy action rescued Chris and his kegs. The shorts were rapidly restored to their proper position whilst he was in transit, propelled at speed by Dad out of the room.

"Can't turn round," thought Dad. "Can't turn round."

The reason he could not turn round was not out of embarrassment but because he was laughing fit to burst.

This joyous event was revisited when chatting with Chris in 2017. Mum said to him that the reason she and Thomas were not apparently there at the time was that she had noticed him just before Dad sprang into action and decided that, discretion being the better part of valour, she needed to get them both out of the room with some haste to be away from the po-faced operatives.

Chris said he felt embarrassed.

"Why ever should you?" and all burst out laughing again at the memory.

A saunter over the Solent

With Chris now twelve years old, the family went to the Isle of Wight for a holiday. Dad had last been there when he himself was knee high to a grasshopper and the group at that time had comprised his parents, older sister, aunts, uncles, cousins and grandparents.

To give an indication of how long ago that was, the trip across the water had been made by paddle steamer.

Back up to date and from the holiday base of Shanklin, there was an excursion to Blackgang Chine, claimed to be the UK's oldest theme park. It's so old that the actual Chine has long since disappeared and, due to coastal erosion, the theme park itself may be on borrowed time.

One of the buildings there housed a potted history of the area, along with static displays and featured boats. Dad is as sure as he can be that one of the pictures on the wall was of the actual paddle steamer used all those years ago when he was still in short trousers. Strange how certain things from an earlier age stick in one's mind.

Chris was exposed to crazy golf, putting and the Dinosaur Museum in Sandown. There was then one event which was all the more memorable because it was one of those shall we – shan't we moments in the car.

"Oh, look, there's a windmill over there."

"Yeah, but it looks closed today."

"Never mind, let's just drop by anyway."

The sign proclaimed The Calbourne Water Mill and Rural Museum and the family made a detour to investigate. This was the only working water mill on the island and dated back to the Domesday Book. There were just a few other people making the same visit, and food and drink was on sale as well as bird seed, even though the mill was not in production that day. After a good look around, Chris wanted to try out the bird seed, not, you will understand, to consume but to distribute.

Well, even accepting that the plethora of colourful peacocks and peahens, chickens and pigeons would have been used to human interaction, Chris began feeding the peacocks up close and personal without reservation or inhibition. Just standing perfectly still he was soon wearing a whole crew of pigeons on his head, shoulder, arms and hands. One was perched on the palm of his hand with the head so far inside the paper bag of seed, there seemed to be more of the bird inside than outside.

Toot – Toot!

Steam engines hold an interest for almost everyone. From the point of view of the more mature person, nostalgia no doubt has a lot to do with this, but why so much for the young? The noise, the smell, the anticipation of going on a journey, the smutty train driver, the even smuttier fireman hauling coal from the relatively cool coal tender to the hot fire in the boiler, the man with the flag, that thick cardboard ticket tightly held, the con-rod wheel drive, the shiny engine, the shout "All aboard!" followed by the "Wheep! – Wheep!" from the whistle as the latent leviathan draws slowly away from the station with its heavy load. However, this is digression.

Toys of any kind are important tools for learning as one is growing up. Chris had great fun trundling his wooden train and carriages all over the carpet and round and round on those sets of wooden rails which can be built into any number of layouts. Perhaps he felt in control.

Thomas the Tank Engine and his adventures on the Island of Sodor were always a favourite with Chris. He loved playing with all the engines and having stories about them read to him from the Rev W Audrey books. He would look forward to the popular animated stories on the television, with Ringo Star doing the narrative from 1984 to 1986 for series 1 & 2 and Michael Angelis from 1991. The cinema film was seen numerous times (six and counting), and the theatre stage show attended. But, of course, all the engines had numbers on them.

Real life heritage train outings were to follow with days out and trips on the Mid Hants Railway Watercress Line, complete with Fat Controller, and trains running between Alresford and Alton. There was also the twelve-mile steam train trip on the line up from Swanage through some lovely Purbeck countryside past Corfe Castle. Next time the family plan to get off at the station for the castle and do some more exploring. There was the whole day visit to the Didcot Railway Centre, the Living Museum of the GWR (Great Western Railway).

Then there was the weekend summer coach trip up to Birmingham which included a day out at Cadbury World in Bournville. Fascinating to see how chocolate is made and to view the history behind it, then make the obligatory stop in the shop there for provisions. The weekend took in Stratford upon Avon (Shakespeare, Ann Hathaway and all that), and Warwick Castle, plus a ride on a real steam train, the *Shakespeare Express*, from Stratford upon Avon into Birmingham Snow Hill station on the Sunday.

On another occasion there was an early morning start for a

day trip down to the Swindon Museum of the GWR. These train stories themselves could cover a whole separate section in this book were space available.

Chris enjoyed the spills and challenges of the original series of *Gladiators* in 1992. He sat with the family to watch the TV shows even though this was as far removed from the altogether gentler world of Thomas and his tank engine cohorts as could be imagined.

Going on a cruise for a holiday was contemplated. Well, there were certainly many and various cruises to choose from and it could not be denied that, by definition, such a holiday would present Chris, even in his most adventurous and exploratory state of mind, with efficiently defined borders. That is, just as long as he doesn't try to swim for it. Not a good thought.

One reluctant...the other less so...

Case 1: Mum took the two boys to see the Bodger and Badger show at the New Victoria Theatre in Woking. Upon arrival, Thomas, wanted to go into the theatre straight away to see the show. Chris was far less enthusiastic and simply did not. This created somewhat of an impasse. The healing balm of gentle persuasion appeared to work as he weakened and then acquiesced. After all, he may have been thinking that if he could not trust Mum who could he trust? He came out after the show saying he really enjoyed it...D'oh!

Case 2: Mum was in Legoland with the two boys who by now were well familiar with the layout of the place, and keen to revisit their respective favourite rides and features. Chris was, as ever, wanting to revisit the pizza concession as a priority.

The Dragon ride in Legoland is an altogether different ride to the one of a similar name mentioned earlier at Chessington World of Adventures. This was a twisty turning roller-coaster type of ride in, out, up, down and through an ancient castle conveniently built to coincide with the opening date of the establishment of the ride. Thomas wanted to go on the ride and, in the way that only children can be, was indeed most anxious to proceed without delay.

Chris was really rather less keen to commit to this endeavour and had his most reluctant face on. Mum's balm was therefore called into action once more. (Really must try to produce some bottles of that stuff!)

He came off the ride in a state of pure excitement. Totally unabashed, he went over to a complete stranger, another mother standing with her own child by the ride's exit, grabbed her by both forearms, looked her straight in the face and declared that this was the best ride he had ever been on. Here it looked as if he had allowed himself to be challenged and had lived to tell the tale. (Again, these days you can check the ride out on You Tube at your leisure.)

CHAPTER SEVEN

Where Do We Go From Here?

So your child is autistic.

What do you do now?

Whatever you do...

"Don't panic, Mr Mainwaring."

"Keep Calm and Carry On."

Noble sentiments; but the family had a way to go yet.

There is no definitive way to bring up a child and no single book giving all the answers, so shared experiences and plans are very useful. Rather like a mutual brains trust.

People would be kind enough to ask how Chris was getting on. This led to some interesting conversations over tea, coffee or even a glass of the appropriate tincture. The question that invariably arose was:

"What will happen to Chris in the future?"

To which the response would usually be, in unison:

"We have absolutely no idea. We cannot think of that. We just go one week at a time and any progress in his development and prospects is strictly on that basis."

There was no other meaningful way to say it. This was not meant to stop or deflect conversation nor was it really a means of defence, because they liked to think they were fundamentally optimistic and constructive about Chris and his situation. It was just that to devour the elephant in the room was going to take time and be on the basis of bit by bit. There was a lot of learning to do.

One week at a time

The formal side of Chris's educational life started with the nursery of Clewborough House/Cheswyks, a private prep school. Then there was the early placement at The Grove, a state primary school. This led on to somewhere that was to prove the absolute making of him, Freemantles in Chertsey. This state school catered solely for the needs of pupils on the autistic spectrum.

Still one week at a time

After Freemantles, in the 2003 school year, Chris went on to Carwarden House in Frimley. This was a senior school catering for children with a wide range of disabilities, not just those on the autistic spectrum.

At Carwarden House there was a definite ethos of discipline. Chris was now plugged into this and everyone was concerned to see how he would cope. There was an established routine but every care was given to the abilities, development and aspirations of each pupil. This routine gave some confidence to the precept that the 'one week at a time' philosophy could now be stretched somewhat. However, there was still the matter of a much talked over parental concern.

"Yes – but what of the future?"

Future hopes notwithstanding, it remained to be seen what impact the events and available opportunities encountered along his path would have on Chris.

Chris was becoming more self-confident, independent, self-disciplined, increasingly interactive and responsive. This was indeed work-in-progress. Whilst having an innocent attitude born of his disability, it was rare that he would allow himself to be or to feel intimidated in any situation. It just was not in his nature. Happily, he was not then, nor is he now, an arrogant, aggressive or malicious person in any way shape or form. He remains an information hoover for facts and data, having an apparently insatiable voracity for knowledge.

CHAPTER EIGHT

Clewborough, Cheswyks & The Grove

Chris Statemented: *In 1997 (for the duration of his school life).*

Thomas, being the first-born child, had the full attention of his mother during the day and the hope was that he should get the best possible start in life. At the age of three he attended the early-years reception class at Clewborough House Preparatory School in Camberley and progressed well.

This school originated in a large converted house in the Camberley area, being originally the site of the headquarters of the Free French Army during the Second World War. A housing development within the immediate area had taken over a large part of the grounds, resulting in the Lower School and Nursery amalgamating with Cheswyks, an existing school in Deepcut and becoming Clewborough House/Cheswyks.

Chris then attended the nursery at this amalgamated school every morning. The staff were good, kind, attentive and clearly really cared about and for their charges. The intent was that at the age of four he should move into the Main Reception Class, but a half-day trial in June proved to be a disaster.

When the head of the Lower School became aware of Chris's diagnosis of autism, her reaction left everyone in absolutely no doubt that there would most definitely never be any future for him at that school. There followed a major consultative meeting between the school hierarchy, the anxious parents, and an extremely concerned but pro-active educational psychologist, all together in a school meeting room. The upshot was that Chris would be allowed to remain in the nursery for a further year until he was five years old...at a cost of course.

This was totally unsatisfactory to the parents and the following day, the educational psychologist's secretary actually rang the parental home to say that she had never seen her boss so angry at the school's reaction. She reported that he would be doing everything he could to help Christopher enter the state educational system...and, thankfully, so it was to prove.

At the beginning of the school year that September, Chris started in the Early Years class at The Grove school in Frimley with a one-to-one helper from the start. This helper was of great benefit and support to Chris in terms of his attempts to assimilate and understand the process that he was now part of.

With Chris now in the state education system, it was felt that the family would benefit from the support of a social worker from the local health authority. A great idea in principle but of course there are only limited resources available. There was an assessment visit to the family home and a further follow-up assessment report meeting.

The outcome both times concluded with more or less the same observation.

"You are coping too well on your own."

No professional help was to be forthcoming. They were turned down twice in their request for social worker assistance. The family would muddle on regardless.

There was then the matter of attending to the paper-work necessary to demonstrate the case for Chris being statemented in order to support his schooling provision. An essential but time consuming exercise requiring an almost forensic examination of the intent behind a whole host of detailed questions, most of which were not relevant, within a document of over thirty pages. The appropriate response to the majority of the questions was to cross through the section and write 'not applicable – he is autistic'. Chris was successfully statemented in due course.

The Grove is a local state primary school close to Frimley Park Hospital. Chris attended mornings only in this first year and, having an August birthday, he was the youngest in the class year. However, as it became obvious that his disability needed constant and concerted monitoring and support, it was felt that he should repeat the year, but this time attending five whole days a week. He would then be the oldest in the year.

The family remembers Miss Cooper, the headmistress at the time, saying that Chris suffered in the morning with so many children in the class but in the afternoon, when there were only some twelve pupils, his performance positively sparkled.

Chris was evidently beginning to make some sense of the patterns in his head and the need to try to achieve some sort of understanding of the world he was part of. Was this the start of his mental hard-drive compilation process and progress? Who can say?

Art is used in the early years at school to encourage young pupils to express themselves in ways that language cannot yet cover sufficiently well. Given all the colours available in class, Chris's early efforts at painting were quite graphic in themselves. They were almost exclusively big round swirls of dark brown or black with no particular shape or form, almost as if he was searching for something to say. Only later did this activity develop into a greater variety of shapes and more diverse colours. His frustrations would ease in time. Such art as he would go on to produce would then almost always be through the use of his computer.

Chris did attend the Leavers Assembly at The Grove when he left the school a year later. The first and only assembly he coped with at the time.

In view of Chris's departure from Clewborough House/ Cheswyks, Thomas's first real sacrifice for his brother was that he too was to leave that school when he finished in the Lower School. The family felt that what was good enough for one son was good enough for the other.

In due course Thomas was able to join his brother at The Grove and daily transport to school for the two minors would then be by means of Mum's trusty Nissan Micra. Before Thomas moved to The Grove, there had been the need to deliver and collect two school-age children at two different schools with similar timings. This did present somewhat of a challenge.

A change of emphasis

At one of the meetings held at The Grove about Chris's progress, Miss Cooper felt he would really benefit from moving to a school more suited to his developmental needs at this stage of his life. A view shared by the educational psychologist assigned to Chris's case. This reasoning was understood and accepted by Chris's parents. This eminently valid independent assessment of Chris's needs was much appreciated and they were very pleased and much relieved that there was the offer of a place at the autistic-specific Freemantles primary school in Chertsey.

From the time Chris joined Freemantles, the educational paths of the two brothers would lead in different directions.

CHAPTER NINE

Freemantles & Guildford Cathedral

Chris Registered Disabled: In 1998 (whilst at Freemantles school).

Some mornings, people just wake up fresher than usual, as if what was a concern the day before had simply evaporated. There was a spring in Dad's step as he made early morning tracks for the bathroom and further invigoration. Today they were only going to sort Chris's future out – that's all!

"Well here we go then."

Conventional schools had been encountered before, of course, but it was with no little trepidation that the parents approached the reception area of Freemantles, this special school in Chertsey, Surrey. A warm welcome ensued and it quickly became apparent that here was a comfortable, established, environment. First impressions are so important, and these were good ones.

Yes, it was different in many ways but not intimidating. There was consistent and reinforcing feedback from all of the staff and the parents quickly became comfortable with the evident ethos of the school. There were 140 places at the school, with fifteen teachers and as many as twenty classroom support staff spread over two streams of five classes. Their dedication to the pupils and understanding of their needs came across very strongly.

By the time of the meeting with Headmistress, Mrs Ruth Buchan, they were already rather won over by the school. Mrs Buchan had clearly already read Chris's brief and outlined what could be done to help him in his primary school years. She was balanced and rational in her approach but quite clearly focused on the needs of those pupils in her charge.

As concerned parents they were impressed by what the future might bring to Chris if all went well and felt this school could make a real difference to and for Chris. Happily the offer of a place at the school was confirmed there and then.

The parents left the school content, relieved and frankly rather emotional, because finally it seemed someone really understood Chris's situation. Freemantles would be good for him. Ruth Buchan proved to be both an inspiration and inspirational. She was to be no less than the air beneath his wings.

Transport to and from Freemantles would be provided by local authority taxi with the lovely Bonny as appointed courier and escort. Now there would be the discipline of a schedule to keep as the taxi would pick Chris up directly from home at the appointed time joining three or four other pupils for the journey to school. The afternoon reverse trip worked in similar fashion. This was a great help and a much appreciated local authority funded benefit. This mode of transport was to continue for a period after he moved on from Freemantles.

Bonny was a mature lady who took a great interest in her brood and discharged her responsibilities with all due care and attention. Indeed the family still exchange Christmas cards with her to this day.

Chris started at Freemantles in 1998 and was to spend five years there.

On his first day at the school, Chris did not feel able to attend the morning assembly, even with the encouragement of the staff. This reluctance could have been from insecurity on the basis that there were a lot of people there he did not know, the new noises, the strange smells and the unknown and unexplored environment not yet being part of his measured experiences. No matter. He was to achieve so much in the future during his time there.

Safety first

Not long after he started at the school, Chris reacted with particular concern regarding the prospect of fire or an open flame in any form. This included matches, gas cooker rings, cigarette lighters, bonfires, barbecues and candles. The reference to candles is particularly relevant as this was another reason why birthdays presented a challenge at home (think cake!). The living room gas fire at home with its open hearth had to be replaced by an enclosed, electric flame-effect fire to part mollify his concerns.

He had evidently been exposed to a safety presentation at the school and Chris, by dint of his condition, would have taken any warning presentations in the quite literal sense of worst case scenario and it is understandable that his initial reaction to all these situations was to treat them as representing the same level of severe risk.

It was many years before he become less sensitive to all fire-related criteria. He had become more understanding of the relative criticality of the range of prospective fire scenarios. This is what nowadays is conventionally referred to as a personal 'risk statement'. He had been warned and he had learnt about it and, from it, developed a worthy and healthy respect.

At home he would react to open scissors drying on the draining board by closing them on the basis of his perception of safety. The family considered these reactions from Chris's point of view and summarily embraced and supported them.

"Always better to be safe than sorry."
No bad thing.

Further home thoughts

Mum spent quite a while setting up a temporary painting table in the kitchen for the boys. All was well until a wasp flew into the kitchen. There was a shriek from Chris who threw up his hands, thereby discharging a large amount of dark blue paint from the pot in his immediate vicinity.

By the time the paint had made contact with the wall, the floor and his brother's hair, Chris was upstairs and heavily engaged in one of his electronic games. Boy, could he move fast! Hosing down the art deco 'instant Banksy' on the wall took somewhat longer to achieve. The pine table took on a distinctly blue hue and the offending blue residue in his brother's hair suffered the unkindest cut of all.

Chris moved on from that period so successfully that he would either ask for, or on his own authority, retrieve the battery-operated bug extractor from the kitchen and gather up any flying or walking insect in his room, buzzing or not, planning to discharge it unharmed out of the nearest window. Something he does to this day.

The onset of the Freemantles era was clearly going to represent change. Change particularly for a mother who until now had really been essentially totally involved with, and responsible for, Chris and every aspect of his daily activities. She would now have to demur on occasion to others with their own group or singular responsibilities of helping, caring, controlling and instructing in school time and even with respect to life in general. She was going to have to share him. This gentle pain was unavoidable but the start of a new regime and a widening of Chris's world which he took to with alacrity.

And then the family met Alison

Alison is a friend to Mum. Well that's not entirely true. She is a very, very, dear and trusted friend to the whole family and remains a much valued surrogate sister to Mum. Alison's background is horses. She had ridden 'show horses' to a high standard in the past, but partly through the state of her own body due to wear and tear and the responsibilities arising from the birth of her own son, she felt she could no longer take the risks associated with the vagaries of controlling high-spirited, self-willed beasts whilst being some six feet or so above the ground, sometimes at considerable speed. Yes, you guessed it, her son is autistic. Not only that but he was and is severely autistic.

Alison's story could fill another book completely. She lives in a tied cottage and with her husband, is involved in the care of Arab show horses for a living.

Alison is a most engaging personality. She has always committed a large part of her life to improving the situation, condition and prospects of young people who these days, are euphemistically and generally described as having 'special needs'. This description always rankles with Dad who would prefer the phrase to be replaced universally by the term 'disabilities', which he considers much more appropriate.

Message to the world – "Please note."

The families got to know each other in 1998 after Chris joined Freemantles, when at that time Alison was heavily involved in fundraising for the school.

A northern lass and pragmatic with it, she is very concerned with and about the people she meets in the autistic world but is always unstintingly supportive and constructive. She has spent a great deal of her life supporting autism care and attempting to widen the public's knowledge and understanding of aspects of autism in general.

Alison is not given to flights of fancy but she thinks Chris has an aura around him and about him. No small accolade to be sure but while some may think this rather a Mystic Meg moment, he meanwhile goes on his merry way, smiling a lot. All this and his dimples too.

Assimilation

At school it was considered appropriate that recognition of his condition should be made by means of him being officially registered as disabled and in due course he was added to the Surrey Disability Register for children.

This was not a problem to the family because it was realistically his true and recognised status. It did not reflect on anyone else and it was certainly taken as no discredit to him. Sadly a small number of other parents at the school could not wait to get their children out of a special school and into mainstream education. Conversely the family believed that Chris would get the best possible support whilst he was at Freemantles.

Chris's fine motor skills were not as developed as they should have been. At the time of a doctor's examination of all pupils at the school, it became apparent that in Chris's case he had a medical condition best described as having a rather floppy relationship between his muscles and the skeleton supporting them. The diagnosis was Hypotonia or, in essence, low muscle tone. This was to improve over time quite naturally, to the extent that he grew up to be a very strong young adult, well connected to his body and one who, having grown into his body, would want nothing more than a playful but strong wrestle and tussle with his older brother.

The result of such robust filial conflicts has never been a forgone conclusion, even to the present day, but the end of the exercise comes amid great laughter from both and tickling from the one who wishes to bring the dust-up to a conclusion.

Skiing

The school arranged subsidised skiing trips to Italy by coach for those pupils considered able enough to benefit from the undertaking. These trips were made under the auspices of the Surrey Special Schools facility.

To determine his suitability and possible reaction to this future option, should it arise, the family went on an exploratory weekend skiing trip to Villars in Switzerland when he was nine years old.

With the weather set fair, this was a good short holiday and the first ski trip for both siblings.

The family had just come down on the main cable car lift and were about to decamp from the pod when Chris simply said a number. The actual number was thought to be thirty-four, though by now memory cannot confirm the actual number – it was a long time ago after all. What was all this about then? Well it took time to work out but he seemed to have been counting the number of cable car pylons whilst in the cabin on the way down the mountain!

So the next day the journey had to be repeated with a view to validating this computation. Yes, the number was confirmed. The family realised further development was taking place within his head but as to what and how, well, that could take time to work out.

Happily Chris was indeed able to take up the option of skiing trips with the school in 2002 and 2003. The first one was a real challenge to him in that it comprised a coach trip across Europe to Prato Nevoso in Italy, preceded by the need to almost surgically extract him from his embrace of his mother in order for him to board the coach prior to departure.

The trip entailed staying somewhere completely outside his comfort zone and coping with what would be a totally alien environment, although he was accompanied by a significant number of teachers and helpers. He would be away from the family for over a week and would have to cope largely on his own with almost everything, including what he would and would not eat.

Surrey County Council had part-funded this trip and later, school videos and photographs at the evening presentation to the large gathering at County Hall, the Surrey County Council Offices in Kingston, gave ample evidence that these trips had proved worthwhile.

Targets

Chris would always notice the tiniest detail and on one occasion in class, he was apparently quite vocal in pointing out an error made by one of the teachers. The break-time had been omitted from the timetable put up on the whiteboard. Another sign of his burgeoning self-confidence.

Chris's world expanded significantly during his time at the school. His parents joined the Friends of Freemantles, a charity involved in supporting the school, the pupils and staff and raising funds on behalf of this excellent establishment. This was also a way of keeping in touch with events in general.

Towards the end of Chris's tenure, there was an indication that the school needed to expand to increase schooling provision past the current stage of just primary school education. Knowing the layout of the school at this time, it was apparent that there would be the need of a corresponding physical expansion and after Chris left the school, Freemantles did indeed move to larger premises in Woking.

Chris was to become a very comfortable inhabitant of the school, from initially being unable to attend the first morning assembly in the gym, he went on to undertake Key Stage 2 SATs (Statutory Assessment Tests) in Maths, English and Science. He passed in all three subjects.

This was a tremendous achievement for him and a real feather in the cap of the school. It was the first time that any Freemantles pupil had achieved such a result. The family was very proud, both of him and for him. Not only that, but as far as the maths exam was concerned he sat it at a time when there was an in-service day at the school. Chris was the only pupil there on that day as the date of the exam could not be altered, meaning he had the undivided attention of all the staff to himself at lunchtime.

The story reached home that, far from needing the extra time allotted to him for the exam paper, he left the exam room rather earlier than he needed to. His form teacher asked him more than once whether everything was all right and reminded him that he had plenty of time to go back in and check his answers if he wanted to. Chris was unperturbed since he felt he had finished and was satisfied that he had done what he needed to...and so it turned out to be.

By now it was pretty obvious that logic played a large part in his make-up. To him things were either right or wrong and in terms of pure adding or subtraction there was already plenty of evidence that he almost never made an error in such sums. Multiplication and division were likewise undertaken in due course.

"How do you do it, Chris?"

"I don't know...I just see it."

He became more inclined to listen to suggestions and contemplate answers rather than just saying either yes or no straightaway without having given evidence of any due consideration. This was again part of his development. It was as if he was building up his own library of variables to add to his data base. The family already had ample evidence of his phenomenal memory and ability to recall events from the past with great clarity.

Getting those feet moving

Most people have some understanding of football, be it from the perspective of a player, fan, critic or supporter. Chelsea Football Club had undertaken the organisation of a regional football tournament for schools with pupils with various disabilities. It was held on a large pre-prepared site where there were a lot of grass pitches.

Travel from school meant a coach journey for the whole team, whilst supporters were expected to make their way to the site under their own steam. Freemantles School attended, fresh from the occasional bout of training back in Chertsey. Happily the event was on a warm summer's day, although Freemantles was the only solely-autistic team there.

Everyone had a great time and there was prize-giving at the end of the long day, with prizes, medals and commendations for all. It has to be said that the sight of a team of autistic pupils playing football was quite the funniest thing seen for a long time, in spite of the gentle and supportive coaching from the side-lines.

Their games appeared to progress on the basis of a somewhat unique premise.

"Well, I've kicked it once – now what do you want me to do?"

Rather like a case of "After you, Claude".

Dad played hockey for the NPL (National Physical Laboratory) club in Teddington and had done so for many years. He was one of a sturdy group of individuals who preferred to compete with their opposition on that lovely inconsistent stuff called grass. Not for him the caged arena of an astro-turf pitch. He had made a lot of friends and acquaintances through these games, both home and away, over the years.

The club ran a Saturday morning semi-official, knock-about hockey session on grass in front of the club house in the hope of encouraging toddlers and younger players to develop to the extent that they might join the club in the future. Thomas and Chris were taken along for a few weeks for them to get some gentle hockey practice but Chris played hockey rather like the way he played football. Oh well.

Freemantles had the use of a caravan, or more accurately a mobile home, at the seaside town of Pagham near Bognor Regis in West Sussex, some two hours' drive from the school. Every year each class had the option to go there for a short break, giving exposure to being somewhere totally different and away from home. Away from home comforts, away from parents or carers, away from any pre-established, fixed routine and with the obvious intent of instilling and developing a greater sense of independence and self-confidence. Chris went every year and commendably returned home that first year with the ability to fit a duvet cover – no mean feat.

He was to later recall how he had been reluctant to go on the first trip simply because it meant leaving behind all that he knew and therefore all that was in his comfort zone. He survived, was none the worse and probably much improved by the change of environment.

The school also organised a group to go on one of the frequently held Farnham scout camp adventure-based weekends away from home. Again, the family had gone through the basis of the weekend activities with him a number of times in advance and, in as much as they could, assured him that he would have a great time. Nonetheless, this did not mask the fact that once more here was a challenge and an experience that he would have to be part of before he would know whether he liked it or not. To this day he usually has to try something new before he knows if he likes it, no matter how many times and to whatever depth pre-instruction or advice is given. He has recognition but not necessarily precognition as part of his psyche.

He was dropped-off in Farnham on the Friday and collected on the Sunday afternoon. He would be on his own with the others for the weekend, but obviously subject to the accredited and capable supervision already in place.

For the duration of the scout camp stay, each of the attendees was assigned a buddy, a young scout allocated to give company, guidance and support and Chris reported that he got on like a house on fire with his.

In spite of a full schedule of planned activities, Chris spied a separate high-level zip wire construction almost as soon as he arrived and made no bones about his intent to try this challenging activity. Here again was an insight into his growing self-determination.

He had already decided, without external advice or encouragement, to undertake what might at first sight appear to be a hazardous endeavour. A course of action of which, by definition, he would have had no previous direct knowledge.

Chris appeared to have done his own risk analysis and decided that not only would he attempt it, but that to his own satisfaction, he would again live to tell the tale. Mission accomplished.

Further confirmation of his growing level of self-determination would be found much later when Chris had his very first Greek restaurant meal aged about twenty, and again, when aged about twenty-three, he was exposed to his first curry house restaurant outing. Both times he made his own rather rapid selection from the menu, independently of detailed explanation and suggestions from those round the table. On both occasions he cleared his plate completely, to his own evident satisfaction.

Was this wild guesswork or a deliberate intent based upon some information extracted from deep within his subconscious? Who knows? He has, however, repeated this scenario many times since. From the point of view of someone whose first word to any suggestion at all used to be "no, I don't like it", before he had even tried it, well, this was progress indeed.

To this day Chris does not eat cake, chocolate, biscuits or sweets although he has a particular fetish for fromage frais. He will, however, devour pizza at any time with the greatest of pleasure. He will often call for an 'azzip'. Salt and vinegar crisps are also one of life's great joys to him. All of that very early, very concerning reluctance to at least try new foods, has gradually evaporated over time.

It has been no less than a real joy to follow the progression of his expanding repertoire of food selection and to see the pleasure he gets from eating what he enjoys.

First there was meat in his sandwich, then more sandwiches, potato, pasta (notably lasagne), peas, carrots, gravy, Yorkshire pudding, sausages, kebabs, rice, miscellaneous fish and molluscs, salted popcorn and the Greek and curry house meals mentioned above. A real eclectic mix. A far cry from his earlier dogmatic reluctance to eat hardly anything.

The broad attainment objectives within the well-supported and committed culture at Freemantles, were self-evident and relevant to the needs of each pupil. Priceless progress and a careful pealing back of all those individual layers of onion by precise observation and planning were to reveal Chris as a diamond – our diamond.

That might sound a tad dramatic, but one way of measuring the school's standing is to have to go through an independent rating assessment. Freemantles was to submit to an Ofsted inspection and the result was that the school got the highest possible rating.

By the time they had got into the 'let's try for children then' type of thinking, there were not so many family members left still standing so there was virtually no chance of respite care time for Dad and Mum. With every thanks to Dad's older sister Margaret and the much loved aunt and uncle (Barbara and Alan) for house sitting there were few, if any, options available.

It was therefore with the greatest pleasure they could imagine that one of the Freemantles' teachers insisted that she be given care of Chris for a few days with her own family whilst his parents swanned off for a short break. This had been planned and looked forward to for some time and proved most therapeutic. Likewise, the teacher's teenage son was looking forward to having a much younger opponent for his video game battles. The teenager was to come second in such encounters.

Then to the hospital...a literal reaction...and mind-reading

When Chris was twelve, the family were in the waiting area of the Children's Unit at Frimley Park Hospital. The appointment was in relation to a visit for a planned minor operation for Chris. The parents were necessarily apprehensive as this was the first time Chris was to have an operation and it would constitute a situation, for all good and valid reasons, where they were not going to be in direct control of him. Chris, naturally, was his usual, conventional, urbane, untroubled self.

The circumstances had been outlined to him in earlier conversations. He was therefore happily, and apparently unconcernedly, playing on the available PS1 console there prior to the family being taken on the viewing tour of the Children's Ward.

Other prospective patients and their families were coming into the waiting area on a regular basis, including one father cradling his very young child, who, let it be said, was looking to all intents and purposes like a somnambulant starfish. Chris looked up and said, with his usual lack of volume control:

"What's the matter? Is he dead?"

Whooahhh! – rapid interaction was now called for.

It was easy enough to understand the request for information, made in his conventional but forthright manner, but how was this to be immediately reconciled – and with this dad – and quickly? Happily, order was indeed rapidly restored. The dad with the small child was calmness personified and responded to the evident self-conscious reactions of Dad and Mum by acknowledging the humour of the situation. He then spoke directly to Chris.

"No – no. He's just fast asleep. Believe it or not, he's got a sleep problem."

Reflecting on Stan Laurel and Oliver Hardy and their classic, black and white comedy films of long ago, there was an immediate but unspoken reaction between Dad and Mum.

Says Oliver (with his characteristic umbrage)…

"That's another fine mess you've got me into, Stanley."

Chris (aka Stanley) was evidently unconcerned, but now satisfied, since he had received the answer to his enquiry and duly logged it into his memory. Dad and Mum were still at the "Phew!" stage. Dad, however, was able to stop metaphorically digging himself into a hole in the carpet with embarrassment.

Based on practice and experience to date, Chris's parents were still in the situation where they were completely unprepared for what Chris might take it upon himself to say on any occasion, and how he might be intending to say it. Further practice would appear to be called for. As far as expertise was concerned, the option of evening classes for mind reading was something they might have to contemplate for the future. As to when and where, well, such matters remain currently unresolved.

So, here again, their literal little superstar had made his presence known.

This "Phew" stage had been survived with Chris largely intact but there would, no doubt, be other occasions yet to come. Oh boy! There certainly would.

The Rollercoaster Conference

The family's relationship with Alison had already been established. She, importantly, was a main driver in compiling the content and format for the Rollercoaster Conference. This was a one-day autistic related event at Dorking Halls for professionals in the public services, held in 2003 (if memory serves) and towards the end of Chris's time at Freemantles.

The conference format was primarily of an interactive nature. Opening speeches in the morning preceded the showing of a video where several mothers were being interviewed about the problems of coping with an autistic youngster from the parent's point of view. One of those parents was Chris's mother. The video was intercut with action footage of the youngsters themselves. The impact here was such that, despite there being over 150 people in the hall, the tick, tick, tick of the wall clock at the back of the hall could be clearly heard as the closing credits rolled.

Lunch was announced but the assembled professionals reacted by way of wanting to see the video again. No problem. The re-screening followed immediately after lunch and the session continued with the main interactive part of the conference. Here, with groups of ten or so at each table, sets of predetermined scenarios were discussed in a round-table format under the control of a moderator. Two parents of autistic youngsters were at each table to be called on for background information or clarification as required.

The afternoon session continued with several talks given by parents in attendance and Alison was the lead speaker here. She delivered factual information with great conviction and control in spite of the extremely moving and emotional personal nature of the subject matter.

The object of the conference was to provide insight to the professionals who, whilst necessarily concerned with the practicalities of autism, were possibly not aware of the over-riding and far-reaching impacts of autism on families.

Those who were there were of the opinion that the object of the conference had been achieved. A really successful and erudite way of getting the message across.

An end...and another beginning

In his last November at the school, along with other pupils from Freemantles, Chris was to attend the annual special schools carol concert held at Guildford Cathedral.

Well, this was to be rather more than just attendance. As well as being part of the school choir, Chris was to read the closing prayer from the dais in front of the packed congregation of 1,000 or so people, where standing room only for late comers was the case.

The delivery was given word perfect, clearly, with no hesitation. He had a smile on his face and notably no sign of nerves, intimidation or lack of self-confidence, bearing in mind he had to cope with a microphone as well. By the time he got to the big "Amen", parental handkerchiefs were much in evidence.

So what was the next step to be taken with Chris?

Two-way communication with the school continued to be excellent and there were a range of ways in which the school provided details of Chris's progress. Chris was comfortable there, but it was time for another leap in the dark. Where should he be moving onto and what should he be doing next?

Headmistress Ruth Buchan said that he had made great progress so far to the extent that, on the basis of his academic ability and achievements, there might be an opening for him at Carwarden House School in Camberley for his secondary school education. This again was a school local to the family home, but this time one catering for pupils with a whole range of disabilities, not just those on the autistic spectrum.

A trip was made to the Open Day at Carwarden House to see what was on offer. The way the school presented itself was impressive. With the overview satisfactory, there was then only the matter of a yes or no to consider...bit of a no-brainer really! It seemed a very good fit for Chris at the time and proved to be so as everyone was to find in many fulfilling and positive ways during his time there.

Through the local authority, a separate offer had been made of a place at Collingwood College just off the Old Dean estate in Camberley. This was a college with a much larger intake, in the order of 2,100 pupils. Dad quite liked the college but on the basis that it was one that, in hindsight, had the sort of environment that he himself might have been comfortable with if he had the use of the H G Wells Time Machine.

Collingwood came across as a very presentable college but did not feel to be the sort of place where Chris would be entirely comfortable. John Cope (Headmaster of Carwarden House) and Ruth Buchan were on the panel which would decide Chris's future school. When the next discussion with Ruth came about, she agreed that Collingwood was not appropriate for Chris's needs and said both she and John were of the view that Carwarden House would be the best fit for him – and so it was to prove.

CHAPTER TEN

The Good Old USA

There was a lot going on whilst Chris was at Freemantles. During that time an opportunity arose to expose him to a different environment, though similar culture, many miles from home. He could gain a great deal from such an experience.

Dad had just started a twelve-month contract with an engineering company in the year 2000. Starting a new job is always a challenge. This one, however, was to start in California. Nice one.

Then came the phone call.

"Next Tuesday get yourself to Heathrow, pick up the ticket and get on that plane to Los Angeles."

"Wilco," or similar, was his paraphrased response.

The original idea was for ten days work in Los Angeles followed by completion of the work over the remaining months back in the UK. Well, here's the good news, ten days became eight weeks. The bad news was that the family would be apart for longer than planned, and by some margin.

He was lodged in the Holiday Inn Hotel, a few short miles from the Pacific. The room came with two double beds and this led to him have another 'light bulb' moment. Like most places in the USA, hotels charge by the room not by the number of occupants. He had to play this carefully, so during one particular midnight call to home (Californian time), he said:

"Is there any chance you can get out here for a short spell with the kids?"

At work the next day he got the email saying that flights were available, with timings given, and good friend Bob available as the taxi service.

"Book it!" was his curt response and he signed off abruptly.

He acted that way because he knew that gave this most resourceful of women all the ammunition she needed. If she booked it quickly, only afterwards would she have time to think about the advisability and practicality of actually undertaking this nerve-racking but splendid endeavour when Chris was only eight years old. This again came under the heading of one of their "Why not?" moments.

That it was necessary to have a safe flight goes without saying. Virgin Atlantic was the chosen carrier in the belief that they would be particularly mindful of Chris's needs. So it proved to be. Their superb Special Needs Assistance Division were care and consideration personified. Chris was at that time still quite in the lack-of-muscle-tone stage and he was provided with a wheelchair and escort through security and onto the plane at Gatwick.

They travelled on 11th November 2000 (Remembrance Day) and rightly paused at the appointed hour in the airport with everyone else.

This was not actually Chris's first time on a plane because he had coped well enough with the earlier short-haul trip to Villars flying from Gatwick to Geneva. But this was transatlantic travel and a much bigger deal by far. How would he cope with airline food? How would his body-clock cope with the time difference?

Dad was waiting in the Arrivals Hall at LAX (Los Angeles Airport), keen to see the family. He was aware that Chris was to have the use of a wheelchair and that this might delay their appearance. Then there was the loudest shout imaginable.

"Daddy!"

This undoubtedly caught the attention of almost everyone else waiting in the Arrivals Hall. Chris had arrived in his assisted wheelchair and on seeing Dad he rose, like Lazarus, from his wheelchair to run across the concourse and fling his arms around his dad. A welcome like no other, a very enthusiastic one, which Dad could see brought smiles of understanding to the faces of many of those standing there.

The Thorpes were together again. They crossed the road into the car park and were in no time at all driving down the coastal freeway towards the hotel. The travellers were very tired, but soon to perk up after some rest and recuperation. They had coped well with the long direct flight. This would be Chris's first experience of jet lag. On the way down the freeway Dad's mind wandered back to that film, *The Railway Children*, and the way Jenny Agutter greeted her dad (Ian Cuthbertson) at the end of the film through a cloud of steam after he got off the train. Granted, the scenario was slightly different but the sentiment felt profoundly the same.

A really rather special holiday of choice

The year 2000 had gone and it was now 2001. As husband and wife, with just themselves to please, the provision of a holiday in the past simply involved selecting a suitable beach-based location for sharing their precious free time, insulated from the day to day rigours of working for a living. However, when Dot & Carry, (sorry…Thomas and Chris), came into the equation it was a different ballgame altogether. Holidays, in as much as could be afforded in terms of time and cost, would have to be more configured in content until the boys were older.

The short-notice Californian experience had gone well and was still fresh in the mind. Where would the family foursome like to go this year if they could stretch to it? Somewhere that Chris in particular might really get a lot out of.

"Hold on! We can't really go back to America – can we?"

The "why not?" question was followed in short order by the "well, we're only young once" point of view. So there it was, a view conveniently held but the consequences of which might not necessarily be so easy to put into practice.

Florida had been the location of choice for their honeymoon in June 1988. Those who have been fortunate enough to go there will have an understanding of the wonderful environment on offer.

In 1988 they had taken the opportunity to act like a couple of semi-responsible adults there – well kids really. Was there a chance to go back and show it to their kids in December 2001? Not only that, but to have Christmas and New Year there into the bargain? This could be a really great dual endeavour.

So, the 'why not?' question having been posed, it was only natural that the 'shall we?' should be trialled. Balance is necessary in any materially important parental discussion and this one was to be no different. What was at issue, however, was just how long it might take to confirm a joint agreement. By any fair margin of error, the duration time of the discussion was less than a nano-second. They were to be on their way.

From personal experience, the feeling was that America appeared to be more accepting and accommodating of autistic people and altogether more tolerant and inclusive. As a young country, America offers a welcome to all, being less judgemental of difficulties and differences. This is a colossal generalisation, of course, but Chris could just possibly feel quite at home in this environment.

An advantageous short-notice deal was secured for the holiday, partly due to consequences of the horrendous outrage of the 9/11 attacks on the World Trade Center and elsewhere. Perversely, the thought was that this would have been one of the safest times to fly transatlantic, but in fact the family actually flew out of the UK the day after the shoe-bomber was caught!

Within the time constraints related to making the arrangements, they delayed telling Chris about the impending holiday. In fact they left it to less than a week before the trip, telling him on the day school finished for the Christmas break. This was a very big mistake.

So much for making it a lovely surprise. Chris was distraught. He was no less than completely terrified at the prospect. He was in tears and absolutely inconsolable when the surprise was broken to him. Here, in hindsight, Dad and Mum might have been understood to have cancelled Christmas, which was a celebration he had grown to know, love, and greatly look forward to. He was not to know that several Christmas presents were to accompany the party and that, in effect, there was to be a second Christmas following the family's return home.

The family was brought up very sharply here and had learned a very important lesson. It should have already been self-evident but was lost in the excitement that they were feeling in going back to somewhere really quite special and magical. They had that pre-knowledge and awareness and, like many others, were prepared to accept the whole environment of the Orlando area for what it was. Chris did not. He had nothing against which to measure the content of the planned holiday.

They would ever more be mindful of the manner in which surprises should be revealed in the future, to the extent that they should not actually be presented as surprises at all, but rather as properly considered pre-surprises.

***

Onwards...onwards

Virgin Atlantic's office at Gatwick had again been pre-notified of the family's request for special help regarding Chris's situation. The airline's care was exemplary and nothing was too much trouble for them. Formalities were efficiently and smoothly dealt with and the appropriately increased security screening at the airport duly satisfied, all in the company of a Virgin operative as his carer.

Seemingly in no time at all the family were safely established on the aircraft and the adventure could get under way.

The self-drive SUV (Sports Utility Vehicle) was picked up on arrival at Orlando airport and Chris threw up in the back seat of the car just after the party had left the airport. The residue was attended to, the window opened, and the family continued the relatively short journey to International Drive, Orlando, in the 'Good Old USA'.

On the first excursion the next day, the family arrived at the Disney Magic Kingdom facility ticket booth and proffered the previously organised doctor's letter regarding Chris's disability. No problem. The arrangement was that the whole family was entitled to an exit-pass. Essentially this allowed all suitably qualified people and parties to present themselves at the exit barrier of almost all rides and individual attractions and access them without having to wait in long queues.

This is a common and welcome practice at Florida attractions and is obviously of great benefit to those who qualify. At no time was there ever an issue with any of the attendants or staff on duty who were only too happy to oblige and provide assistance and support where needed. Nor was there any indication that this was seen as a point of issue by any members of the public.

There were many other families making use of this arrangement. This was seen as an entitlement and not the seeking of an unfair advantage. What a refreshing attitude.

Unfortunately Chris had picked up a bug before the holiday which was to lay him low over Christmas Eve and require the restorative powers of a pizza on Christmas Day by way of recuperation. An interesting and unplanned Christmas Day meal for all.

A New Year's entertainment

Being mindful of the hiatus regarding late notice to Chris of the surprise Florida holiday, there was now another hurdle to overcome. A booking had already been made for a Pirates Dinner Show just a little further up International Drive from the family's holiday base. Now, fair enough, it was for New Year's Eve and of course the family had the choice to go or not to go, though the cost of the prepaid tickets had been quite high.

Attendees are usually there for the entire evening and, as well as committing to the entrance fee, there are other revenue -raising events on site for the duration. However, there is usually the choice in these sorts of places to spend or not to spend. If the evening was not thought good value by those attending, the attraction would soon go out of business through word of mouth. This show is still in business as of summer 2018.

This is America and by and large they do give a choice after all.

The family did have a most enjoyable time there and, that being the case, it would be only right to say it was good value.

There were many guests enjoying pre-show snacks and being entertained by magicians and conjurers passing through the crowds, plying their trades. Everyone was waiting in the rather dark and gloomy assembly room, before the arena doors were opened. Yes, it was noisy. Yes, there were a lot of people there.

Chris had undertaken the short journey there with trepidation. He had generally given the impression of being unsettled and unsure in spite of the encouragement from the rest of the family who were rather more excited and enthusiastic. Within the assembly room there was understandably a fair amount of noise and it was indeed rather dark, but Chris munched on some of the food on offer anyway.

A Tannoy announcement gave the rousing count-down to the opening of the arena doors in the way that can only be done in America. The doors to the auditorium duly opened with a flourish and Chris simply turned tail and ran with intent in totally the opposite direction.

"Oh lordy," was the thought.

"What's to do now?"

He was quickly and carefully apprehended and, because most of the people had by that time already gone into the arena, he listened to the gentle enticement.

"Trust us, Chris. Just come with us to see what it is all about and we can leave if it is a real problem for you."

As soon as the family walked into the arena Chris's inhibitions simply fell away at the sight before him. Here was a pirate ship with masts, rigging, sails and netting, sitting in a lagoon.

Spoiler Alert...Spoiler Alert. Those pesky You-Tubers and their videos were not around at the time that the family went there, but can now be accessed to give an understanding of the scale of the enterprise. The view from the perspective of a rather vulnerable small boy was just like going into the biggest toy shop in the world to see a floodlit auditorium replete with a replica of a fully rigged eighteenth-century Spanish galleon, measuring some 46 feet long, 18 feet wide and with 40-foot masts, slap bang in the middle of a 300,000-gallon indoor lagoon. A magic moment.

The audience was seated in sections, each related to their own area of the ship. Each section had its own designated mascot pirate leader who was to represent them during the show. The family attained their preassigned seats and the entertainment began with lots of shouting, hollering and Yo-ho-ho-ing. There followed stunts, acrobatics, pyrotechnics, romance, humour, the whole kitchen sink in fact. Dinner was not epicurean, but pleasant enough. More entertainment ensued.

American shows like to involve a measure of audience participation, not just on the general level of being harangued from the stage, but by individual involvement.

This Pirates Dinner Show was to be no different and made for what was to be an enthusiastic finale. During dinner, a number of the servers were multi-tasking by passing through the audience asking if some of the youngsters would be prepared to be conscripted (or as would be understood in the UK, press-ganged) to take part in the show. Chris's eyes lit up in that entreating way that most boys can use to demonstrate pleading and in spite of, or because of, the drama before the show it was a no-brainer to agree that he should have a chance to have a go at whatever was to come.

It would be known soon enough whether he might be intimidated or confused by such an inclusion.

He was collected during the intermission and at that time a further invitation was offered in respect of Thomas. He had previously made every effort to be cool and aloof but at the same time was obviously intrigued as to what was afoot with his brother. Actually he was gagging for it. Minds had to be made up quickly.

"Well, what's good for one should be good for the other, Why not?"

"Go, Go!" and the boys disappeared.

Towards the end of the show things were becoming ever livelier on the galleon. Chris and a small number of others, all in uniform, appeared in a dinghy piloted by a pirate, rowing round the ship and appearing to reconnoitre the goings-on aboard as they passed surreptitiously round it. Then at the finale both boys, in company with a number of other suitably clad Redcoats, appeared on the quayside armed with rifles which, on cue, they discharged in the direction of the pirates to cut them down and win the day. Great fun.

After the show, everyone was to enthusiastically count in the New Year back in the large anteroom. The family then chose to walk back to the holiday accommodation on what was a balmy very early morning – by UK standards that is. Chris was roundly greeting complete strangers in a rousing, exuberant, and uninhibited fashion.

"Happy New Year."

He was full of vim, vigour and good cheer. The responses came back to Chris, in turn, with equal goodwill and in suitably fond manner. What a turnaround for the family. What a turnaround for Chris.

Shopping...plus other distractions

Holiday shopping in such an environment is something that simply has to be done. Just ask Mum. In America not only do they make it easy for people to go shopping, they are very good at getting people into the shops and malls in the first place. They make it too easy. Just ask Dad.

In one of those malls the family was out together and, as ever, mindful that it was a good idea to keep an eye out for Chris if he should stray. After what was surely only a momentary lack of attention, he had done another runner.

The party of three on round-up duty found themselves in

one of those Disney stores where the branded merchandise was freely on display. Chris, in his period of freedom had taken a liking to one of those battery-operated toys of Mickey Mouse and Donald Duck on a sled. He had found the pressure switch in the foot which set this toy into action. Well, that's not exactly true, because he had actually set some twenty-five of these toys into action simultaneously and was highly amused with, and entertained by, the whole exercise. And...and...was going round restarting those that had gone back into sleep mode, much to the amusement of the shop assistants.

"Time to move on, Chris. Time to move on."

One of the attractions on the west side of International Drive was Race Rack, a lively, busy, popular eatery and alcohol bar, featuring Nascar and Formula 1 cars on static display and with many and various TV screens showing car racing action, interviews and the like. This is America and you cannot get away from TV screens. These sports bars are everywhere, although recent research shows sadly that this one has since ceased trading.

This was a great stop for lunch but what lay right next door provided much more food for thought. It was a helicopter pad.

Hands up all who remember the Whirlybirds black and white television show in the late 1950s. Dad's in danger of giving his age away here, but still remembers Chuck and PT flying around in their Bell Jet helicopter. There on the pad was a Bell Jet helicopter sitting for all the world like a goldfish bowl on skis complete with tail. The helicopter was in work, providing a bird's eye view of the surroundings to customers prepared to part with a measure of cash for the privilege of ten or twenty minute pleasure flights.

This chance would not come again, thought Dad, but first he and Mum needed to talk to each other, then to Thomas and then Chris. Whilst everyone was concerned, with Chris naturally and understandably the most nervous, he did in the end yield. Harnesses secured, helmets on and with microphones activated for the pilot's commentary, lift off was in two phases. Dad and Thomas for twenty minutes, Mum and Chris for ten minutes. There were terrific views in lovely sunny weather but the concept of looking down through one's feet was rather disconcerting. Everyone survived.

With the large Disney and International Studios theme parks plus Cape Canaveral and all the other big and small attractions, there is simply not enough time to see everything whilst on holiday in Florida. Careful pre-planning is the order of the day in order to focus on the must-dos, against the nice-to-do-if-there-is-time type of activities. It is easy to be cynical in such an environment but, if parents can get down to the level of being children for the duration, then there are magical times to be had.

One pre-booked event entailed a car drive to a separate Disney hotel for the Mad Hatter's Breakfast. Food was provided in the form of a large, repeat large, buffet. But then, Americans are quite often large themselves. There were some twenty tables each with twelve or so place settings. A range of Disney feature characters and cartoon characters would visit each table, nod frequently, shake hands on demand, embrace all who elicited an embrace, pose for photos and, of course, say absolutely nothing.

Every so often the characters changed tables. Evidently the plan was that all breakfasters were to have time with each character on parade that day. Dad's favourite was Snow White. The whole thing was run very professionally and it was as if there was a sprinkling of magic in the air. Chris enjoyed the whole experience very much.

One of the rides at Disney's Magic Kingdom is the 'It's A Small World' boat ride. Here a flotilla of dinghies travels an established, automated path through shallow water into a large atrium area where painted plastic dolls joyfully sing the sugary sweet song, and sing, and sing, and sing to exhaustion. Chris enjoyed this hugely but the rest of the family tolerably so. Well that was the first time. It was such a twee slow boat ride.

Chris wanted to go round again and again to the extent that in the end, parental sanity was up for grabs. That in itself perversely made it a fun event for the family.

"Never again!" was the thought that came to mind at the end of this activity.

Current You Tube videos of the ride, not available back then of course, sum up the situation concisely. Have sympathy.

This chapter is sounding rather like a travelogue and substantially understates the value that Chris got out of all the activities and the nature of his involvement with them. Even so, mention simply must be made of the Universal Studios & Islands of Adventure facilities towards the top end of International Drive. They are well worth the trip, especially if there is an interest in film related topics, associated activities and simulators.

Mention had been made earlier that The Simpsons was one of Chris's favourite TV shows. Imagine then the reaction when he found out there was a Simpsons Ride in the theme park. Let it be said he was extremely pleased, and that is putting it mildly. Of course, he went on it more than once.

Chris was deadly accurate with the water hose at the Sponge Bob Square Pants sideshow game and won the prize, a large sponge cushion model of 'Bob' which Dad had to carry for the entire day. He also particularly liked the Toy Story ride, collecting shooting points from his transport through this gentle ride. There was the Will Smith – Men in Black ride, much faster and disorientating but with similarly significant scoring by dead-eye Chris. The Jaws ride is sadly no longer available but at the time comprised a hosted search for said shark at speed in a multi-seater launch over water around Amityville and proved quite exhilarating …the list goes on.

Seaworld is another worthy attraction. It was wonderful to be right close up to the dolphins over the pool wall. Perhaps next time there really could be the chance to swim with them. Feeling the top of a Manta Ray revealed a texture which was rather like that of a front door mat. See the Orca whale show. (Sorry – no can do. It is discontinued.)

The not so subtle message, 'Exit through the Gift Shop' is ever present. At almost all rides and shows one has to pass through the sales area when leaving that feature. This requires the exercise of significant willpower to avoid succumbing to the temptation to buy one or more of the related items on sale. The family usually gave in and bought at least something by way of a souvenir. Chris, no doubt in training for his own fully independent fiscal future, usually found something to take his own interest.

Colorado skiing

About as far away from Florida as one can get lies Colorado. This was to be the subject of a later, separate, holiday to America for Chris in company with the family. Chris had already been skiing with Freemantles in Europe but now it was to get really interesting. Dad had been fortunate enough to go skiing with friends several times to an area some one and a half hours west of Denver, the mile high city.

Driving an SUV up Interstate I70 found the family at a place called Breckenridge, which is a great hub for a whole range of ski resorts within a short ride thereof (such as Arapaho Basin, Keystone, Copper Mountain, Beaver Creek, Vail, with Aspen a little further afield). Breckenridge is by USA standards an old town. Mining had been the reason for the original development and it can be more than a tad busy on occasions in the town. The main street is some 9,600 feet above sea level and the various slopes go up from that general area. Lots of skiing is available with the runs not nearly as crowded as in Europe, due to the sheer expanse of available slopes.

The skiing areas in the States are truly vast, generally very well organised, as safe as can reasonably be expected and efficiently policed by a whole range of locals suitably empowered for that purpose. However, the USA, whilst offering great freedom does so within a litigious environment. Be safe; be careful; behave.

One of the reasons for choosing Breckenridge was that it had a facility described as the Adaptive Ski School. Research from home identified this and a similar facility at Keystone, just up the road, as offering a personalised service and customised skiing and boarding programmes for people with any kind of disability. They cater for blind skiers and boarders, cross-country skiers, physically disabled people and, notably, people with autism.

Arrangements were made from home in advance along with payment of dues. When Chris turned up on the appointed days he would be set up with all the necessary ski gear and go out on the slopes with a suitably qualified and registered person as a combined tutor, mentor and trainer for skiing lessons on a one-to-one basis.

This was a risk for the family, but one thought worthy of taking. It might be a real bonus for Chris to be in such an environment, with only minimal contact with the family until lunch time and when the lessons finished for the day. He was to be on his own. The people in the organisation were wonderful and hugely committed to the cause. Chris indeed flourished and found a new self-confidence. That he had great balance was never in doubt but he was shortly to demonstrate that conclusively on his skis.

The rest of the party had just finished lunch and were about to set off on one of the Blue slopes down from the Ten Mile Station restaurant on Peak 10. Chris had joined the group outside the restaurant after his morning stint of schooling and there was conversation in the air. He was perched on the slope in the correct manner, across the line of the slope, quite stable, relaxed and comfortable.

"Time to move on," said Dad.

At which point Chris jumped his skis round competently, thereby facing directly down the slope, and did no more than just take off down the slope with skis parallel...straight down the slope...that is, really...straight down the slope **and with no ski poles to be seen.**

With all this talk of the USA, there was one other place in America that appeared to warrant some attention on behalf of Chris and his love of numbers. I wonder. There is always Las Vegas. If anyone remembers the film *Rainman***...well!**

CHAPTER ELEVEN

Carwarden House

Chris had already made great progress thanks to his formal education at Freemantles and the family's long-distance travels. The next step was the move of the formal side of his education from Freemantles to Carwarden House. It proved to be seamless.

It was easy to be drawn into the world of Carwarden House as concerned parents supporting their son. Their involvement led to committee membership of the Friends of Carwarden with Mum co-opted as Secretary and scribe. Topics discussed were many and various and it was interesting at these meetings to be made aware of future developments regarding the school and the overall plans on behalf of the pupils. The school had an inclusive atmosphere with everyone contributing to the greater good of the pupils.

One concern was how to support and improve Chris's eating habits. He would close his mouth whilst eating and had always done so. This was very polite, but was he actually chewing the solids he ate or simply swallowing them? Looking at him very closely it did not seem that he was chewing with his molars and it was not at all clear that he was biting or chewing with his front teeth either.

A referral to the Orthodontic Unit at the Royal Surrey County

Hospital in Guildford to investigate his teeth and jaw configuration in 2005 provided remarkable evidence that there was indeed a problem, but one which was capable of correction. The inside of Chris's mouth had not previously been subject to summary investigation and there was concern that this might provoke some reluctance from him in order for the consultant to gain entry.

Thankfully the consultant had been pre-warned that Chris was autistic. He proceeded to tell his patient in detail all that was planned for him. This worked like clockwork. Congratulations to the doctor. Chris even allowed teeth moulds to be taken, twice, with that horrible soft plastic stodge which even adults find unpalatable and uncomfortable. The whole procedure went well and without even a glimmer of demur. Well done, son.

The eye-opening result of the radiograph of his jaw showed the full extent of the problem. His upper front teeth were of the order of 45 degrees to the vertical. Dental practitioners might describe this as an overbite but if so it was a mighty big one. No wonder Chris did not bite, he could not actually do so. However, he would not have known anything different of course. The consultant said that he could help and he praised Chris whom he described as a model, tolerant, patient. Chris was to be fitted with adjustable braces for his teeth, just like his brother, and both boys would take it in turns to play act as if they were the Jaws character out of that James Bond movie.

Chris was also found to have one adult tooth orientated at virtually 90 degrees to where it should have been in the gum, (i.e. horizontally rather than vertically). This tooth was to serve no useful purpose and it was going to have to go. An operation under general anaesthetic a short time afterwards solved that little problem. Again…all part of the learning curve.

Actual cleaning of his teeth was never a problem for Chris even with all that clinker in his mouth – praise be for battery-operated toothbrushes. After several check-up appointments at the hospital and with the local dental practice on hand at home, progress was effective and the time lapse until his bite-was-right passed soon enough in 2007.

His reconfigured teeth improved his choice of food and he ended up with only a very modest overbite. It may be that he had known all along that he could not actually chew solid food. In any event he got his own back on the consultant at the hospital because by the time Chris had finished with him, the consultant knew all there was to know about the wide world of Pokémon.

Carwarden House Headmaster Mr John Cope, a lovely man, was dedicated to the care, attention, wellbeing and progress of his pupils within a disciplined yet constructive environment. One of the many other committed teachers was his wife Su, who was to recognise a feature of Chris's ability which she undertook to develop to the extent that he would progress beyond levels thought appropriate at the time. He was going to do mathematics, hopefully at GCSE level.

The thought that he should even be considered capable of entertaining any understanding of algebra as a subject was indeed challenging, but everyone was up for the challenge. He applied himself valiantly, but the concept of absorbing the need for 'x' and 'y' variables to be combined in such apparently strange ways was as alien to him as it may well have appeared to so many others. Perseverance led to partial perception and enlightenment but it was a problem for him to understand just how and why algebraic equations worked and what their use could be related to in real life.

To his credit, he continued this work longer than he might have done for other studies because there was something in his make-up that meant he would usually 'know' a subject immediately or not. The 'not' seemed by him to be very important to the adults, and so it was, with the benefit of that perseverance, that in June 2008 he passed GCSE Maths with the grade of 'E'. Amazing. Here was something to be celebrated and able to be built on.

Socially he got on well with almost all his peers at the school and, though happy enough to enter into amenable group meetings and discussions, this would usually be on the basis of a request or direct invitation to him rather than him seeking such group company. Fund-raising events at the school such as the occasional film based horse-racing betting evenings were OK for him and he would be seen tucking into the fish and chips or chicken and chips with great enthusiasm.

Discotheque evenings were more of a distraction and he would go outside the hall of his own volition to avoid the impact of what to him would be very loud music. He was not alone in that respect but did not always need to seek the quiet room provided at the school for just such eventualities.

Academic activities for him were well up to speed. However, in terms of PE (Physical Exercise) work, he was reported as valiantly contributing to cross-country sessions by stoically running around the perimeter of the fields of the school during the keep fit lessons. He was evidently never going to come first but he would dutifully apply himself. To this day, out of choice, he prefers the company of his own mobile games console and computer, both of which remain largely stationary and under his sole control.

Another feature of the school was the regular open-evening event. Here, form teachers were arranged behind desks in the combined gym/assembly hall and by previous appointment, parents were able to spend a preassigned ten minutes with each teacher responsible for their child's education. Some parents took up more than their allotted time for this exchange than others, on occasion thereby reducing these evenings to the concept of a rugby scrum or even speed dating. However, these gatherings were actually a much valued way of receiving direct parental feedback and as there were only a prescribed number of pupils at the school, everyone was able to have their say in due course.

Biscuits and soft drinks aided the constructive atmosphere.

Developments...

Carwarden House provided the first real independently measured notification that Chris had become a resource. He was to become a prefect and had a nice shiny badge as confirmation. Dad had been a prefect in his own time at his own school (it has to be said ...many years earlier). Now they had even more in common. Dad and Mum were so pleased that he had been considered worthy.

Chris was assigned a buddy organised by a local organisation, Link Leisure (now re-branded as Linkable), in Woking. Chris already knew him from an earlier Saturday morning football club held for children with disabilities, he being one of the organisers and a carer to boot.

This buddy was actually one of the classroom assistants at the school, supporting the class teachers, taking some of the workload and providing general one-to-one support for the pupils in class. He wondered if it might be a good idea to take Chris out occasionally, giving him someone different to relate to, with different ideas, outlook and conversations closer to those of his own age.

These extra-curricular social activities proved to be not only a great idea, but worked really well and Chris got a lot out of them. The pair of them would go ten-pin bowling, to Marwell Zoo, to Birdworld and elsewhere, travelling by car, train and bus. The cinema was a particular favourite and, although not actually needed for Chris, the Camberley cinema now provides special screenings catering for those on the autistic spectrum.

Naturally enough, he was also to meet a whole new set of fellow pupils at the school and two in particular remain firm friends today. They are James and Patrick. Patrick, being aka BFF,

Best Friend Forever. The family gently teased that he also had a girlfriend, but he constantly chided.

"She's not a girlfriend, she's a friend who's a girl."

The Lion, The Witch & The Wardrobe was a three-act school play with each act performed by a different class at the school. Chris was the narrator for all three acts of the play. When asked, he used to say to the organisers that he preferred not to actually be an actor.

He had the script open in his hands but did not once refer to it. He proceeded without hesitation or prompting of any kind throughout the entire performance. Again…remarkable evidence of the capacity of that brain of his. He had once more proved he had an impressive ability to assimilate, record and reproduce large amounts of data and information. The family insight to his memory abilities was growing significantly.

On another occasion he would volunteer to organise and work the lighting rig of another play put on by the pupils rather than be an actor in the play himself.

There were weekly work-experience visits for the older pupils to Brooklands Technical College in Weybridge. These were formulated on the basis of giving direct exposure to a range of possible future work-styled placements. The pupils were exposed to various vocational courses such as retail, hairdressing, vehicle maintenance, horticulture, painting and decorating. Each taster session lasted six weeks and was for just one day a week.

By some long-lost reasoning, Chris undertook the horticulture session, but this was evidently treated by him with some measure of disdain. Exposure to the rather messy activities related to potting shrubs into flower pots was apparently tolerated to a degree. However, upon the requirement to shovel up some horse pooh in order to serve by way of garden manure, he did no more than 'down tools', refusing to be coached any further in this task. Happily no sanction was applied but, hey, a demonstration of such character is surely worthy of note and to be celebrated.

There was a sixth form facility at the school, vested in a separate but close-by building within the school grounds. Here a number of the pupils would gain further development, education and guidance at the end of their period of statutory education. Chris was not to take up a place here because his future was to lie in a different direction.

Chris's involvement in this tremendous school and the constructive and non-judgemental environment was to end all too soon. Suddenly the Leavers' Prom loomed.

A suited and booted Chris, accompanied by the rest of the family, arrived for the mutual meet-and-greet reception. There were some fine words from the podium by Headmaster John Cope to speed the worthy on their way to their own futures in the world beyond Carwarden House. Snacks and soft drinks were gratefully devoured and a myriad of snaps taken amid all the nervous energy.

This energy was quite palpable. Parents, guardians and the pupils themselves were understandably and naturally apprehensive of what the future might hold for them in so many different ways.

Prior to moving on to the Leavers' Prom, a group of parents had foregathered for a small pre-prandial session at one of the parental homes with their smartly dressed progeny. The idea was to see their offspring depart in imposing and previously organised hired transport, in this case a stretch limousine. The parents would then make their separate ways to the Prom at the school.

Chris was invited to try some champagne before departure to the Prom.

"No thanks I don't like it," was the automatic reply.

This was a strange repost from someone who had, to the best of everyone's knowledge, no past history of such a libation.

"Go on, it's your leaving do and time for a toast, it really is a very special occasion."

Without further comment, he leant forward to accept the offered glass and consumed a modicum of the contents.

"Mmmm!"

He then took great delight in downing the remaining contents in rather swift order.

"Nice," he said.

So pleased was he with this result that he took a second glass with similar consequence and declared himself well pleased once more.

"That's nice, Chris – well done and that's quite enough alcohol for one day."

What a way to go.

CHAPTER TWELVE

Brooklands Technical College & More

2008 to 2011:   *Brooklands Technical College Supported Learning Unit*
                          (Barclay Building)
2011 to 2014:   *Brooklands Technical College (Main College)*

Here there was to be quite a change to Chris's routine.

The Open Day at Brooklands College prior to the academic year 2008 enabled the place to be given the once-over by the family and allowed Chris to get some understanding of the facilities and information regarding the individual courses and classes available. Brooklands was to be his preferred college selection.

He had been offered a place at Farnborough Technical College but he was already familiar with Brooklands, having visited there on a weekly basis from Carwarden House. That, along with the thought that a number of his peers from Carwarden House were also to go there, probably swung the balance in favour of Brooklands.

One further observation at the time was that the special needs facility at Brooklands was a self-contained establishment in its own building – the Barclay Building. This was a separate feature on the Main Campus whereas the comparable facilities at Farnborough were not as segregated, being in the same building as the main college. Farnborough may indeed have done as well for him, or even better, but who can say?

The family had now reached the stage of being able to look ahead for longer than just one week at a time. Now it was time to think in terms of at least one year at a time. Definite progress.

In 2008 Chris started as a student in the Supported Learning Unit of the Barclay Building at Brooklands College in Weybridge.

For the first two years, transport to and from college was by local-authority-funded coach travel. The college coach had a designated pick-up point at an appointed time in the village, fortunately within walking distance from home if necessary. The system generally worked quite well, though Dad or Mum had to occasionally fill in to provide transport by car directly to college in the morning, or to pick up from college in the afternoon. This was not usually a problem provided earlier phone calls gave notice of the appropriate arrangements and pick-up details.

In order to be able to make and receive phone calls, Chris needed to have the use of a mobile phone of course and, most importantly, he had to know how to use it to be able to contact home as and when necessary, especially as he was to be that bit further away from home during the day. He was given his mobile phone, contact numbers were installed, trial calls made, trial calls received until familiarity appeared established. He would have the ability to phone home to let people know where he was and that he was safe and he could advise if there was any change of plans at the college.

At home, there would also be some certainty as to his in-transit status during the first two years of funded coach transport so that if for no other reason the coach drop-off time in the village could be anticipated. For the subsequent years at college this was even more important as the coach transport facility was withdrawn and Chris had to travel by train, needing him to be more self-reliant on his phone in order for him to be picked up from the station.

As long as it was not mislaid, the phone was to prove an invaluable tool. It was now part of his everyday existence, putting him in the same position as most young people of his age. It was a good interface plug-in for him.

He took management and the discipline of coping with the responsibilities of his phone in his stride, keeping an eye on the level of charge, charging it when necessary, turning it off in lectures, turning it on again after lectures (initially a challenge for him), keeping it in a secure pocket, downloading relevant 'apps' etc.

Like most youngsters his relationship with the mobile phone has grown to the extent that it is an intrinsic and well-used constituent of his communication skills. He would be almost lost without it and, consequently, the only valid means of separation of one from the other nowadays would appear to require surgery.

Chris started off in the Barclay Building, which catered for students with disabilities within a structured, supported learning environment and classes were therefore smaller in number than would have been the case in mainstream college. This gave the staff the facility of closer interaction with individual students and greater attention to their varying needs and abilities than might otherwise have been the case. So this was a secure environment but with a significant level of personal freedom within which to support the students.

Daily residency in the Barclay Building was usually set at two years duration. Whilst he was comfortable there, it was apparent and accepted that it would support his academic progress and his all-round development if he stayed on for a third year.

Consequently by the time he entered the main college in 2011, he was two academic years behind where he might have been in mainstream education, but for his autism. In some senses he was effectively only one academic year behind, on the basis of his birthday being on 27th August.

There was one very concerning occasion regarding the transport arrangements in the first year when, at the end of the autumn term just before the Christmas holidays, Chris phoned to say that the coach had not arrived at college to pick him and his mate up at the end of the day.

It was quickly confirmed that there would not now actually be a coach available that afternoon as it was stuck in traffic on the M25. The boys were stranded. Darkness was setting in, it was raining, college buildings were being locked down for the holiday period and Chris's mate was not quite as able to cope with this disruption, becoming increasingly anxious and concerned. Yes, there was a degree of panic in the air but what was to be done?

Dad was at a function in London and Mum, with no satnav and no sense of direction, had no idea how to get to Weybridge in the rush hour and in the dark. Dad would, however, acknowledge that she is practically flawless in all other respects. Dad?...Dad! ...where are you?

Yes, Weybridge train station was within walking distance but at that time Chris had not yet had the opportunity of travelling independently, especially by train.

How would he know when and where to get off the train, even accepting that he could organise both him and his friend to buy tickets and get on the right train in the first place? By the greatest of good fortune a student in the main college, living in the same village as Chris and known to the family, was also stranded. He took charge and got the three of them safely to the train station, onto the correct train and back to the village, to be met by grateful mothers. Crisis averted.

This incident subsequently resulted in a number of concerned and concise emails and calls to the main college at the start of the next term regarding the fact that these vulnerable boys had effectively been abandoned on site at the college.

Here was a prime example of just how useful mobile phones

could be because Chris was able to be contacted and told what to do. He put up with the whole hiatus and saw the arrangements through. Always very capable when he is on-task.

As mentioned previously, at the end of the second college year the local authority funding for the transport arrangements was pulled. How was Chris to travel to and from college now? Clearly travel by conventional bus was inappropriate and impractical. The journey would be some twelve miles by road and in any event, be of an unrealistic duration. Personally funded taxi journeys were discounted as not being feasible from a cost point of view. A train journey was called for and the challenge then was how to arrange it.

Chris's buddy from Freemantles days was contacted and only too pleased to be able to help. He was subsequently commissioned to undertake a range of dry runs to and from Weybridge station with Chris in the holiday period for him to gain familiarisation with the whole situation. This would include, but not be limited to, ticket procurement, train timings, ticket etiquette, who to talk to and who not to, how to contact station staff, care of his student rail card and means of payment by both card or cash if there were ticket problems. The family was most grateful for this mentoring.

With no little parental concern, Chris started to travel to college by train at the beginning of the new college year. He was driven to Brookwood Station in the rush hour to get on the one direct train to Weybridge, from where it was but a short walk to Brooklands College. Mum retained responsibility for actually buying the train tickets and both she and Chris were to become avid researchers of the train timetables.

Whilst on the train, Chris was obviously out of direct control and supervision but he usually took solace in the machinations of his handheld games console for the duration of the journey. On one occasion he was so engrossed that he actually overshot his target of Weybridge station. Unperturbed, he simply got off the train at the next station, had a word with the station staff and went over the bridge to catch the train back to Weybridge. He was even able to get to college in time for the start of the first lecture. Fortunately he only told his mother of this at the end of the day so earlier panic was averted here by default. Good for you, Chris.

At the end of the 2010 to 2011 summer term and therefore in his last year in the Barclay Building, Chris and his parents attended several evening 'open working sessions' at the college where students were exposed to presentations showing various follow-on possibilities and given some indication of what jobs might be available in the local community if they were not going on to further study.

These evenings provided useful insight as to what the next steps might be for students moving on from college. Chris, however, would be staying on to move into the main college on the same campus.

Parents were also invited to attend the class end-of-term play, performed by the students in the Supported Learning Unit. The play segued two popular films of the time, *Hairspray* and *High School Musical*. Reluctantly, but with characteristic stoicism, Chris played his part. Not sure that he got much out of it though.

Chris was awarded an Edexel BTEC Level 2 Diploma in Workskills and an Edexel BTEC Level 2 Diploma in IT (Information Technology) with the grade of Distinction based on completion of his year 2011 work in the Barclay Building. These awards, which were actually officially issued in 2012, formed the basis of him being able to progress to the main college for further study in the 2011 to 2012 academic year.

His grades for the seven IT scopes of work involved were as follows:

Communicating in the IT industry	Distinction
Working in the IT industry	Distinction

Computer systems	Distinction
Database Systems	Distinction
Website development	Distinction
Computer graphics	Merit
Spreadsheet modelling	Distinction

Upwards...

Time now for the move into the main college at Brooklands. There would be little, if any, of the very close care and attention provided in the supported learning environment of the Barclay Building. Now he was to be out in the real world, not quite all on his own, but not far off it.

The Open Day prior to the academic year 2011 to 2012 for the main college, specifically the computer-based study options, saw Dad, Mum and Chris clambering up the stairs to the 7th floor of the building where the computer-based courses were held.

Lecturer Mike Andrews took every care in giving a comprehensive overview of the computer courses, the computer facilities and the various syllabi available. This sounds rather like a collection of alcohol-based creamy fruity desserts, not the plan at all. Mike Andrews had come into teaching from outside the academic world giving credence to his brief review of the possible job prospects available for students after leaving college.

He went on to say that the courses for which he was responsible appeared to attract quite a large proportion of students on the autistic spectrum. This indeed seemed to be a good fit for Chris's latent computer-based abilities. Dad and Mum just looked at each other – this was where he might very well be happily occupied. Mike then mentioned that recently one of his students had actually gone on to take a university degree. Dad felt the hairs on the back of his neck rise and was sure that Mum had felt a similar tingle at the time.

Mike Andrews was to have a big impact on Chris's studies and prospects from the time he left the Barclay Building and moved into the main college.

Brooklands College was a technical college for those passing through the tertiary stages of the education system and catered primarily for those interested in vocational skills. Some (just some) of the students there gave every impression that they were only there because they could not or would not fit in elsewhere, did not want to go out and get a job, or did not actually want to go to university.

They were the students who were generally more visible in the social sense with an apparent lack of direction or self-motivation. This rather sadly set them apart from the majority of the intake who gave every impression of being there to work, to get on and really achieve something.

It would not have been difficult to identify Chris at college as one who, by virtue of the manner of his walking or occasionally apparently preoccupied nature, was someone who was different, possibly even vulnerable.

Chris was walking across the campus one day when a girl called out to him from the small group she was with, no doubt hoping to gain kudos by embarrassing him in front of the group, making a number of comments about his clothing in a manner best left to the imagination. Chris, of course, does not suffer embarrassment or intimidation. He would have given a totally neutral projection of his body language, exchanged names and given every impression that he did not understand the innuendos (which he probably hadn't anyway), and simply made some innocent small talk in return.

The outcome of this was that, in future, when Chris saw this group again, they acknowledged each other as acquaintances with no malice intended in either direction. Someone had learnt a lesson.

When he was at the main college, he would take his pre-prepared lunch (generally sandwiches, a banana, a packet of salt & vinegar crisps and a drink) into the refectory for consumption.

Chris came home one day particularly keen to share some news.

"Dad, today I got something beginning with 'D' and ending with 'N'."

There was a glint in his eye and he was absolutely bursting to impart the information. Dad looked at him dispassionately and responded immediately.

"A dustbin – what do you want with a…!"

"Noooohhh!" came the strident howl.

"A distinction!"

Pause for laughter and many congratulations.

"Proud of you, Chris and so very pleased for you. Good work. See what applying yourself can bring."

People at Brooklands interacted with Chris on many levels and with various responsibilities during his time there. The family always tried to let those in charge of him know the appreciation felt for the consistent, caring and committed support given to all of the students.

Chris, in his outgoing way, also particularly wished to record his gratitude to Mike Andrews (leading the computer section), Annette Preece (the 'IT Queen') and Janet Jones (his main tutor).

Chris was to retake his Maths GCSE exam, giving him the opportunity to improve on the previous level of Grade 'E' achieved at Carwarden House. To his own great satisfaction and due in no small degree to his hard work, he achieved a Grade 'C' level, a notable improvement. Much joy.

Although he had never sat an official English exam in his life, now he was going to have to take one at GCSE level, which in itself was a challenge. If this went well in terms of a result (Grade 'C' or above), along with the Grade 'C' in Maths, here was the final gateway to being able even to consider the possibility of going to university.

"University – for heaven's sake!" thought Dad and Mum.

For the end of his studies at Brooklands in June 2014, he achieved a BTEC Level 3 IT (Information Technology) Diploma with 'Double Grade Merit Merit'.

The progress and successful conclusion to this part of his studies was achieved by Chris due to his own commitment. He had recognised a target, wanted to achieve it, felt that he could achieve it and by the end of that time had achieved it.

He was to leave Brooklands with a near perfect 100% attendance record with just one late attendance caused by unavoidable transport problems due to South West Trains.

His grades for the twelve subjects were as follows:

Communication & employability skill IT	Merit
Computer systems	Pass
Information systems	Pass
Organisational systems security	Pass
Digital graphics	Merit
Impact of use of IT on business systems	Distinction
Spreadsheet modelling	Merit
Software design and development	Merit
Systems analysis and design	Merit
IT technical support	Pass
Project planning with IT	Merit
Database design	Pass

Yes, University was a distinct possibility.

"What the heck do we do now?"

But fear not, help was at hand. Oh, and before the seeds of doubt are sown, be assured that his parents would like to stress that they believe they are as far from being pushy parents as can be imagined.

Chris was keen to try for a computer games or IT-based university placement if at all possible.

If he was not offered a place or it was considered that he would not be able to cope with the challenge of the curriculum and the life of a university student, well then at least everyone would have tried their best and it was not to be...but it was to be.

So, at the end of this period of study at college this very special young man had just qualified to go to university.

"Wow!"

Would he like to try for university?

"Yes."

Well – here we go then.

The possibility had grown to probability and now to actuality.

Confirmation of the offer of a BSc Honours Degree University placement for the year 2014 came from UCAS, the Universities and Colleges Admissions Service, based on his Brooklands qualifications. This notification was followed shortly by details of the disability-based support available at Kingston University, this being the university, location and course content of choice. Even greater joy.

So then to the 'More' section of this chapter

Detailed research was undertaken to investigate alternative study options which might be available for Chris should he not actually be offered a place at university.

Merrist Wood College, close to Guildford, was visited. This is primarily a vocational farming and animal husbandry establishment which, although it might subsequently enable entry to Guildford University, did not appear to be relevant to, or of interest, to Chris.

Although he was charmed by the animals being cared for on the campus and would have no doubt been content to learn all about them as part of the academic side, it was immediately apparent that his preferred choice of games or IT courses of study were not available here. The visit was interesting but the college was not an appropriate fit for him.

A confirmed appointment was made for a visit to Esher College. Here, regrettably and irritatingly, in spite of making their presence known, the family was kept waiting for an hour and a half after their designated appointment time without even an apology before anyone came out of the ether to attend to them. This was doubly disappointing as Dad will always attempt to be early for an appointment rather than just in time.

As soon as Dad and Mum walked in through the front door, however, they had actually formed the opinion that this place would not do for Chris. He was not going to go there and nothing they subsequently encountered during the day came even close to convincing them to the contrary.

The family left the site at the end of the day intrigued as to why one of the questions directed towards Chris during his assessment, required him, or even his mother come to that, to know which year women got the vote!

"What the hell has that got to do with the price of fish?" was the comment between the parents as they approached the car for the journey home.

An offer of a Diploma-based IT course was subsequently made to Chris but by then his future was thankfully to lie in an entirely different direction.

Chris actually received offers of a place from the two universities which had been under consideration both for him and by him. The explanation behind the final choice is worth relating.

The choice of university for computer games or IT studies for Chris had been rather limited. There had essentially been a choice to make between Kingston University and Guildford University. Both offered appropriate courses and both were within a reasonable distance of home. Chris was in the situation where living the conventional university student life in Halls or rented accommodation away from home was not an appropriate option for him. He would need to be able to travel from home on a daily basis.

In terms of Open Days at the prospective sites, Kingston appeared the more appropriate of the two. The Penrhyn Road campus was ordered, compact (but not cramped) and a number of lecture theatres were manned by people giving in-depth explanations of various courses and the nature of university life.

Chris was comfortable with this on the day and was given guidance on the level of student and NAS (National Autistic Society) support available to him as and when needed. He also had great fun trying out the Occulus goggles in the well-appointed computer laboratory under the guidance of an assigned buddy on the day. This buddy was a student already doing a similar course, who was partnered with him for the time the IT lecturer explained the course content.

The Guildford campus by comparison appeared rather large in concept and content, having to cope with over 23,000 students. On the day, it gave the impression of presenting a rather unfocused attitude to the specific needs applicable to Chris and students like him. Such information and details as were presented did not sufficiently or satisfactorily explain the level of any available support for Chris, let alone the content of relevant courses.

Due to significant planned building development work at the main Guildford campus, it appeared that his classes would be at least part held in the university canteen. For the whole duration of the visit, the person responsible for interviewing the family and making presentation of the Guildford facilities never made eye contact with Chris at all and certainly never engaged him in conversation.

Both universities would give transport concerns for Chris but lingering reservations regarding travel to Kingston University were to be satisfactorily resolved.

The choice between the two universities was therefore a bit of a no-brainer for him. As he might be imagined to advise, somewhat loudly:

"Kingston wins the tourney!"

(By way of clarification, tourney means tournament.) His idiomatic expression is quite apt though since it is just what he does. It is what he is.

Welcome to the warren that is the Royal Holloway College

Chris duly accepted the offer of a place at Kingston University and contact was made with student support there, specifically the Disability Support Section.

He was evidently entitled to a certain level of funded support for this stage of his study life and an appointment was made for him to undertake a Disability Allowance Options assessment meeting. This was to determine the nature and level of support available and applicable in his case. The assessment was to take place at the Royal Holloway College in Egham, Surrey.

This impressive building is to be found on the right-hand side of the road when travelling north on the A30 towards the always busy M25 motorway. It is a totally unmissable structure, with an external chateau style of architecture reminiscent of St Pancras railway station.

The building is part of the University of London and at this time comprised nineteen academic departments. Dad, Mum and Chris, fresh with his confirmation of a university place, attended as appointed.

The parents approached this meeting with rather more trepidation than Chris who was operating on an ignorance-is-bliss basis. The invitation was actually extended only to Chris, he being the subject of the exercise of course, but they hoped it would be appropriate for them to sit in at the far end of the room as observers to cater for any point of confusion or lack of understanding which might arise during the meeting.

So with Chris and Caroline, the assessor, plus computer at one end of the room and parents some way away at the other, it began. Chris is a most engaging and uninhibited personality and he reacts in a natural and unconcerned manner, especially in one-on-one situations.

"I wonder how long it will be before he has her wrapped round his little finger?" said Dad.

Caroline was most professional in her approach but there appeared to be a correspondingly engaging reaction from her.

She would ask a question and receive a complete response in return each time. Communication was going well and on receiving responses to certain telling questions and little tests, she smiled and let him continue until he had finished what he wanted to say.

At the end of the session Caroline advised that in her opinion Chris was indeed well worthy of support and entitled to certain aids, grants and hardware and software items out of the Disability Budget. Items included, but were not necessarily limited to, a dictaphone, computer printer and sundry smaller supportive items. To this day the Mavis Beacon CD on learning to touch type, remains wrapped and unopened – not needed.

She was able to say that on the basis of this meeting and his responses and reactions he was, in her opinion, not only a suitable student for university placement, but the disability settlement to be offered would be based on her recommendations to the powers that be. Great news.

Caroline was not actually based at the Royal Holloway. She had the responsibility of disability needs assessments for a wide range of candidates and was usually based at Brunel University. The Royal Holloway had ample administration provision and it had been a convenient place to hold the meeting. The support Chris received through her efforts was exemplary, first class, very helpful and very supportive. It has been good to be able to keep in touch with her and report back on his subsequent progress.

Thinking back to earlier mention of St Pancras station, brought back the memory to Dad of the guy who was tagged the 'helicopter autist', Stephen Wiltshire, many years ago. Research into the *Daily Mail* archive, reports that at eight years old he sold his first drawing which was of Salisbury Cathedral, motivating him to communicate with others and giving him the impetus to lead an independent life.

Dad well remembers him being featured on television more than twenty years ago, being taken on a helicopter ride over London and then drawing the façade of St Pancras station in detail, and with great perspective, completely from memory when he got back to terra firma. This seemed the first major demonstration of the media concentrating on such autistic talent in a significant and positive way. That word 'motivation' is a really key word here and the concept of self-motivation is something that Chris has been able to pick up and work with.

CHAPTER THIRTEEN

The Mums' Network

Autistic children have little need or desire to gather in groups or draw their acquaintances close for comparing notes.

Thoughts on school work, how to work the latest electronic games console or what horse is going to win the 3:30 race at Kempton Park Racecourse on Saturday, all tend to remain solitary preoccupations. What would be called social intercourse is not as necessary for them as it is for others.

An important group of people who most certainly do need that sort of communication, however, is mothers (Mums).

People need people

Mums need confirmation of schedule dates for a whole range of variables such as school classes, timetables, travel logistics and the like, plus the not unnatural comfort of sharing opinions on everyone else's children. That's just for starters.

There is a joint interest in the endeavours of their children, identifying and rationalising their lives in terms of school work, home activities and overall development.

Janet and Jane had become very firm friends of the family from the time they, along with Mum, had boys at Clewborough

House, then Clewborough House/Cheswyks. This friendly coven was initially drawn together by a mutual interest in the progress of their first-born children who were the same age. Neither dear friend's offspring was subject to a disability themselves, consequently neither was really aware at the time of the wide scope of the autistic spectrum. A very important aspect of this mutual support and advice was to come all too soon from dear Janet.

When she was given the diagnosis of Chris's condition, Mum did not have her man directly to hand. She quickly upped-sticks and went directly to the lovely Janet. It was good that she was at home and available as she was a no-nonsense type of person who was the ideal support at this difficult time. She was pragmatic, supportive, intelligent, helpful and concerned, all rolled up in the one persona.

This was a most therapeutic encounter and, at the end of the day, all Janet had to do was listen – a task undertaken with great care and concern as one would do for a close friend.

In due course and as circumstances unfolded, this was to be the start of a rather wider Mums' Network.

When Chris had moved on to Freemantles, Mum found herself in the situation where she was suddenly surrounded by other mothers who, by and large, were in the same position as her. Such intelligence as had been discovered by one was quickly shared amongst all in need of information. None were to be left to struggle on their own. A truly interactive support group was therefore established where all were there for each other – support for all – a Mums' Network.

This network also served to provide a level of early mutual emotional support, in one sense vital in terms of retained sanity and yet illustrating the shared needs of a whole cross-section of people in similar circumstances. These ad hoc meetings provided an ideal forum for coffee consumption and a review of life changed concerns within convivial company. Some of those mothers have become close, dear, life-long friends.

Even today, the network changes in terms of those who are drawn together and those who move on, retaining contact but not on such a necessary or regular basis. It is a group of friends from school days gone by, united in the activity of talking...talking... talking. With lots of laughs along the way as well.

The need for the network is still there and each is still very interested in sharing contact and the progress, development and achievements of cherished offspring.

Human relationships can be fragile currency. What starts out as a two-headed venture, say, between male and female, entered into with understandable trepidation on both sides, hopefully develops into an adventure. If the basis of the footings are well set then change, compromise and direction are capable of joint nourishment and accommodation and the relationship grows and blossoms but not necessarily always in the pre-planned direction. If couples are so inclined and so fortunate, offspring may appear. This, history tells, provides for a possible all-up-in-the-air set of unforeseen consequences and major impacts on any relationship. Management of such a set of happenings is problematic enough to work with.

Consider then the situation when there are one or more children identified as having disabilities of whatever nature. It is a sad and inescapable fact that at this point relationships with these responsibilities can change and even break down completely, either overnight, or over a longer timescale, resulting in much pain and distress. Alternatively, relationships can take the other path and freely accommodate such change. Going with the flow as it were.

The reasons why there are break-ups in respect of couples with autistic children are too numerous to think about, are rather sad, and generally are of little matter anyway if the break is so brutally final. This would be the time to move on.

Think of parents, by no means special, super or abnormal who, already having what may be described as a normal son, are changed by the addition of a second son. This time an autistic son. They are drawn further together in so many ways by shared experiences, most of them happy ones. It would be appropriate to call them Dad and Mum here because that is who they are. The challenge now is to accommodate the very different needs of two growing children. Game on.

As parents, their decisions are made under whatever set of circumstances are present at the time. They believe their partnership to be a great bond between them. In light of just how much of that load falls on Mum in terms of the children, well that is a heavy load. Thank goodness for the ability to connect with the Mums' Network.

One thing this merry band of sisters provides is the vital ability for mutual discussion of the wider aspects and reasons for the behaviour of everyone else's children as well as their own. Trying to find answers, trying to find common ground, are constant mutual themes. Chris for example, did have the occasional pram/buggy mini-tantrums when he was very small, but was never wilful or disobedient, punching, kicking or otherwise being physically violent towards others, be they big, small, parent, friend or relative. He was not disruptive in any way, possibly due to constantly attempting to make the best sense he could of his immediate surroundings and the world at large.

Interfacing with Work Experience activities

At Carwarden House the pupils were encouraged to undertake outside work experience in term time to widen their horizons, meet new people and learn new and practical skills. This applies to all school pupils of course, although from the disability perspective, this required some particular research on the part of both the school and the parents as to which options might be the most appropriate in each individual case from those available. Much food for thought.

All placements are unpaid. This might be taken to be fair treatment and appropriate compensation for a measure of disruption to the company concerned in terms of standard business practice and corresponding impact on any pre-existing long term training courses.

Retail placements are only of short-term duration but are particularly appropriate for pupils with disabilities since the retail world might well be a realistic option of future employment for many of them. A parental observation here is that making money when one is young is no easier than when one is somewhat older.

Placements for Chris thankfully turned out to be almost universally very successful. The scope of his varied undertakings covered the following:

1. Retail support at the HMV store in Woking. This included categorising and re-sorting racked discs into the required order. Here, this and related activities, benefitted from his entirely logical and efficient outlook.

2. Games Store in Camberley. Retail exposure on three separate occasions. The first two under the supervision of the manager, 'Mr Chris', and the third with 'Kelly' also at the shop.

3. Petrofac Engineering in Woking. A two-week secondment in the IT department exposed him to aspects of the support needed to ensure a company as large as Petrofac has properly validated, fully functional business systems in place to support the varied aspects of their operational existence. He

was to return there for additional sessions on two further occasions.

4. Zavvi. Working on the shop floor.
5. Budgens Supermarket, Lightwater. Unloading and stocking goods in date order on the retail shelves.
6. Freemantles school. Office work, photocopying, collating and other related activities.
7. Surrey County Council (Employability) offices in Woking as part of their employment services for young people. The office staff delegated a programme of work to him, maintaining and inputting attendance records, for a two-hour slot every week for five weeks.

After charming them into submission on his first day there, he proceeded to complete the five-week assignment, the entire ten hours, within those first two hours! Such were his computer skills. The programme of work was necessarily modified by a measure of expansion and he left at the end of the five-week period with no little sense of achievement.

Chris learnt a lot from these activities. The fact that he was to be invited to repeat the exercise at a number of these places, and in the case of Petrofac (a major oil and petro-chemical engineering contractor), for two further engagements, is surely confirmation that he had been of use and to have been of value and no doubt mutual amusement. Reports to the family following these assignments were encouraging, appreciative of his input and often supportive of his uninhibited personality. His work ethic certainly appeared to demonstrate efficiency and expedience.

It was good to be able to share his experiences with others of the Mums' Network. The knowledge gained, experiences, interactions, successes, failures and the hoops gone through were the currency of such continued conversations.

What gets on to television

Another core feature of the joint coffee mornings would be the chance to talk about something of interest that was going to be on TV or which had recently been broadcast. Some autistic related examples are outlined below.

The Autistic Gardener

This was a series of four documentary episodes featuring Alan Gardener. A great character in his own right who has Asperger's syndrome (this being a separate form of autism), and who therefore has little need or desire of small talk.

The first episode aired on 8th July 2015 on Channel 4. He led his novice trainee team, almost all of whom were autists, in planning, designing, configuring and actually achieving the execution of rather stunning, distinctly different, garden transformations. Each garden project presented its own set of challenges but every week the team provided a great result and was able to fulfil the paid commissions from those members of the public who had made their gardens available for the work in the first place. He had a lovely turn of phrase to describe the state of his troops.

"We are not broken computers, we just have different operating systems."

From his own point of view he reported that he sees things rather as shapes and patterns. He also finds it particularly difficult to be provided with myriad options from which to choose, such as might be offered by a waitress in a restaurant...but these are just two aspects of his make-up.

The programmes gave great insight into how Alan and his crew produced impressive and imaginative garden make-over results primarily, by means of application of the principles of mathematics.

He expanded on this by saying that not a lot of people know that mathematical formulae occur in flowers, stamens, petals and leaves and these patterns can be used to create and construct brilliant gardens.

He would also frequently refer to people outside the world of his team of special helpers as neuro-typicals. A very enlightening series of programmes.

In June 2017, at the precise time of writing this section of the book, the weekly television guide was promoting a second series with the aforementioned Mr G. This series was to feature UK projects alongside visits to the USA. The precis described him as '...wonderfully creative and charming' and it would be hard to argue with that. He now carries the tag of being an award-winning horticulturist and evidently still has his bright pink hair and red finger nails. His team this time would not include any fellow autists but would again feature paid commissions.

Man and Beast

Part 2 of 2 of an ITV programme called *Man and Beast* with Martin Clunes included a section on how horses can be used to help autistic children. It was broadcast on 23rd August 2015 at 10:15 p.m.

Michel Roux

The chef hosted a series of TV programmes from the end of October 2015 grouping together Asperger's, Downs Syndrome, autistic and Tourette's Syndrome youngsters plus one blind youngster. The premise was to see if under varying degrees of personal pressure, any of them could achieve the goal of qualifying to work in a professional kitchen by the end of the series.

This really did seem to be car-crash television bordering on exploitation of these people for some misguided sense of entertainment. For this programme to have worked in any way at all there should not have been the need to put them into such a competitive situation.

All should have been able to show that they had succeeded to one degree or another, but then that would presumably have voided the original idea. The whole concept of the series appeared to be wrong.

Such a diverse range of vulnerable people cannot be tarred with the same brush and this just reinforced the view that autistic youngsters in particular have to be treated as individuals. The autistic youngster featured, however, had every right to be proud of his initial success.

Chris's parents were mightily unimpressed and found that altogether rare television button, the 'off' button and took no further interest.

Chris Packham

On 6th April 2017, the *ONE Show* on BBC1 featured Chris Packham, a naturalist, animal man and Asperger's autist. A contributory article on the show featured fourteen shops in Sheffield which would open early in a pre-prepared autistic-friendly environment and interviewed the woman who was the prime mover in making it happen.

A great idea and one which is becoming a more widely used concept, reducing loud background music, strong lighting and crowds of people, all of which autists can find incredibly disturbing.

Chris was called downstairs to see the article, thanks to the rewind capability on the TV box-of-tricks.

"Yes – I remember feeling like that," he said.

It was also evident on the programme that Packham has an affinity with animals – just as Chris appears to have.

Bit of a coincidence here but the same TV listings magazine that featured the return of *The Autistic Gardener* also gave notice of a one-off documentary on Chris Packham, relating to the way in which autism has impacted on his relationships. No doubt most worthy, but the separate review of a controversial treatment that purportedly cures autism will be viewed from a distinctly sceptical point of view.

CHAPTER FOURTEEN

Great Hard Drive − 'Iffy' Interface

It may be hard to believe, but with the possible exception of when he has been unwell which might cause a temporary change in his demeanour, Chris has never ever, woken up with an 'attitude', having a 'monk' on, feeling over-tired, having a 'bad head', a hangover (he does not drink alcohol to any measurable degree), or even with what might be described as just having something on his mind. It is as if he downloads everything overnight to start the new day afresh.

What a great attribute. It is a shame that it is not possible to distil and share that ability.

He used to give every impression of being quite content to be living in the present with no apparent need or thought to the relevance of past or future events.

Now he is aware that he has to know his plans for each future week at university, arrangements for future cinema film viewings with family, BFF (Best Friend Forever) or his buddy, and a whole range of other activities. He does now look forward to particular future events but he remains happy for someone to make plans which he can accept or reject, rather than making too many plans and suggestions himself.

Notable exceptions here would be particular television

programmes he wants to view as a family and his dear wish to be able to go to the Anime Games convention weekend at the London Metropolitan University.

Now and then he will come out with a memory jewel from the far dim and distant past to the total amazement of his parents. This can include the precise time and date of such a memory, whether it be a significant one or one thought to be of lesser importance. What makes the link for Chris to have that connection, to have that recall, is a matter of parental work-in-progress.

The thought is that Chris is able to access parts of his brain as an autist that are inaccessible to those who are not autistic. Whether this is pure conjecture or recognition that this is the brain compensating for the misconnection, fouled state, or merely the failure of certain neural pathways is for more scientific minds to study. It is, however, an accepted fact of life that it is not at all uncommon for one or more of the five main senses to intensify application, sensitivity and reactiveness to compensate when one or more of those senses is compromised.

Jigsaws are used with young children to introduce them to handling, matching, connecting and building pieces together in their simplest forms. Early puzzles are usually made of wood with bright, varnished, patterns and greater dexterity with age leads to more complex puzzles, instilling the concept of building a bigger picture from a collection of small cardboard pieces to achieve a result comparable to that on the cover of the jigsaw box.

As far as starting a reasonably large jigsaw is concerned, it is usually good practice to cut down the variables by sorting out the four corner pieces and then all those pieces with one straight edge. Now there is a chance to compile at least part of the border and go from there. But not if you are like Chris.

In spite of several coaching sessions, he was not one to garner straight edge pieces, let alone trawl through the box to find the corner pieces. What he would do, however, on more than one occasion would be to pick up two or three pieces apparently unrelated to the picture built so far and merely place them arbitrarily within the framework of the jigsaw being constructed by others and then retire to his gaming upstairs.

Intriguingly, it would often be found that his pieces were very much in the correct place, waiting to be joined up to the developing picture in due course. This appears to be further evidence to support his view that he thinks of solutions in terms of pictures and almost instantly at that. No edging or corner construction for him!

The American television show *CSI* (Crime Scene Investigation) had several offshoots based on specific locations in the USA. The *CSI* of choice at home was *CSI* Las Vegas. Many moons ago when the laudable Grissom was still head-honcho, an episode featured a story line where one of the main characters was an autistic librarian, bright as a button and evidently very intelligent. In one scene, Grissom is questioning the said individual and, having deduced that he is autistic, asks him if the answer is that he sees things as pictures. The response was in the affirmative. This episode has always stuck in Dad's mind.

Asking how Chris actually arrives at his own solutions does not usually illicit a fully coherent response…well, one that the family can understand anyway.

How does his brain actually work? Dad and Mum often muse on this and at the end of such conversations will commonly reduce the analysis to a simple whimsical observation.

"Not a Scooby Do." (Meaning 'not a clue'.)

The need of study to try to understand and communicate with Chris and his brain remains.

Logic plays a large part in his make-up. That much is obvious, without doubt. It is a realistic comparison to make, but his brain really does appear to resemble a computer hard drive. However, interpretative skills and abilities are still developing and evolving as he matures so that part of his persona remains another work-in-progress.

It is as if he has to continue to learn. He is like a sponge, always seeking new input. Everything that goes in stays in and he is blessed with a tremendous retrieval system and a photographic memory. He makes more and more sense of things himself these days, surely at least partially due to the ever increasing cross reference of stored experiences he has logged to date. Aligned with this is the fact that he is very observant and simply notices everything. This is no doubt helped by his heightened senses.

He is constantly evaluating his parameters and expanding his world and abilities as he goes. With this mainly mental development comes a greater measure of the level to which he is able to understand, demonstrate, and vocalise emotions. This is another standard challenge for autists. Back in 2016, when at home he quite simply and out of the blue said:

"Mum, Dad, I love you."

What a thing for him to say. The parents reached for the tissues.

He has the ability to process large amounts of data very quickly. It is also not entirely fanciful to believe that his brain actually operates at a faster response rate than others. As a first thought that might sound a rather unrealistic observation, but to continue the computer analogy here, essentially his 'read' rate is higher than his 'write' rate. This can make for an interesting time when he is particularly keen to get his point of view across because he will start talking like a machine gun. He will then realise he is talking too fast for all his words to come out coherently and deliberately pause as if to let his audio interface catch up, whilst he himself attempts to modify his verbal discharge rate. Even now this is a common occurrence when he is excited.

He does tend to over-analyse things. In computer speak this could allude to the need to go through all the variables before collating something worthwhile to transmit. He is getting better at trialling output for discussion with family and people in general and then organising his words when he has refined the limits of the discussion in his own mind. By such means he can entertain what anyone might simply describe as normal conversation. Whatever anyone wants to call it, he really is getting better at it. That thirst for knowledge is unbowed, as if by acquiring more and more knowledge he has the chance of a greater understanding.

Back in August 2015, round the dinner table, there was a rambling conversation with Chris regarding just how far he might be able to go in considering intelligence and knowledge as separate criteria. This, on the pretext that knowledge ('K') can be learned, given, or stored whilst intelligence ('I') might well be just a measure of what is intrinsically there all the time and in simplistic terms, the thread(s) that bind all those neural pathways. The parents were trying to get Chris to know himself a little more, but not get too overly concerned about the point at which the lines of knowledge and intelligence cross, only to understand that to get the best results, there should usually be a mixture of both.

Bearing in mind his perceived speed of thought, particularly in relation to exams, the intent has been not to pressurise him, but there was the need to point out that when in the exam room he should take the time to read the questions very, very, carefully indeed. This to ensure as much as is possible that he fully understands what is being asked of him. It is easy enough in the real world to go at it like a bull in a china shop and not only go off on the wrong tack, but actually not even answer the questions posed. Chris had, and still has, to be particularly aware of this.

Computers operate best under consistent operating and atmospheric conditions. Chris is simply a lovely warm body who does not appear to overheat or become cold under any change of environment. He remains pleasantly, if not intriguingly, warm to the touch when in one of his many calls for a family-hug moment.

It is to be hoped that his internal thermostat continues to operate as efficiently in the future.

In the Jim Carrey feature film comedy, *Bruce Almighty*, Carrey's character exchanged places with God (aka the splendid Morgan Freeman), or rather was changed and established as God in place of the good Mr F by Mr F, with no comprehension of the responsibilities this involves. Of course, in the film there are far -reaching consequences for getting what you wish for, because before long he finds he has to cope with everything not just the bits he wants. In one part of the film for example he has to cope with everyone in the world sending in prayers, wishes and pleas for assistance through every means possible: email, phone, letter, TV, internet messaging...you get the picture.

Leaving aside the gentle morality of the film, this does give some allusion to the sort of difficulties faced by the likes of Chris in trying to contend with a myriad of details such as news, knowledge, instruction and interaction, with no personal information filter. Jim Carrey's character could not cope. His whole interface system had, in the vernacular, 'gone up the pictures'. Happily Chris is learning to a greater or lesser extent to be able to monitor and moderate his reactions giving him increasing personal control.

Constructive developments

There remains the matter of programming the hard drive that is Chris. He still needs external input to run his many 'programmes'. In this sense he could be given a general request.

"Put that over there, Chris please," this meaning that a sauce bottle in the café should go back to its original location.

He would often put it somewhere in the rough vicinity and

not necessarily exactly where he should have put it. Any specific instruction or request still has to be exactly that…explicit and precise. Clearly Dad and Mum are still learning this game.

Whilst he is blessed with truly exceptional hearing capabilities, he does appear these days to be able to better filter out those sounds, noises and conversations not actually relevant to him. This has surely helped his cognitive processes and his ability to communicate more effectively and intentionally comes under the heading of being an 'interface improvement'.

His constitution is now physically solid and strong. This is a welcome development from those earlier days when he would become over-tired on long journeys and give every impression of being rather weak and quite wan.

Watching TV used to be a challenge for Chris because he found it difficult to follow a storyline. Now he will sit down with the family to watch something which may have been recommended, or which he has selected for family viewing, or something which just takes his fancy. Apart from his beloved *Robot Wars* and *Doctor Who*, *The Simpsons* remains one of his favourite programmes. It is lovely that he will choose to watch it with the family and it is regrettable that not many programmes have that universal appeal these days.

In April 2017 he was watching a particular episode of *The Simpsons* with Mum and was duplicating the audio in 'real time' without apparent error or hesitation…

"I remember this was on in the plane when we were travelling to America," he said.

That was a long time ago. When *The Simpsons* is on TV he laughs in all the right places…loudly.

Manners...and mannerisms

He is the politest person you could wish to meet and he greets and deals with people in the same open manner – especially if he has not met them before. His parents would not have it any other way and are pleased to take at least some responsibility and credit for the instillation of good manners. What they have little responsibility for, however, is to have someone who has the most engaging personality, is very quick to laugh and who can readily demonstrate an understanding of irony and wit and vocalise superb mimicry all at the drop of a hat. He's done that himself.

He always asks if he can be of help, which is lovely, but he has to be reminded to read all his emails from the university website. He can offer opinions on such communications but not always be fully cognizant of all aspects of the content. This is where he usually seeks out the family for discussion.

He is essentially self-taught in terms of typing, which he executes consistently at a phenomenal rate with an amazingly high degree of accuracy, self-correcting as he goes. His reactions are like lightning. One day it may prove instructive to actually have these reactions measured under controlled conditions. Judging by his scores on the many and various electronic games he exposes himself to, his response times are being maintained at very high levels.

There is another aspect of the matter of 'neural pathways' to reflect on. Fundamental research continues to reveal more and more about the brain and how it operates but, even now, little is known by the lay person about the intriguing details of this absorbing operating system. Taking the way in which the brain transfers and shares information, the manner of data transmission would appear to be a largely consistent model, otherwise there might well be a fundamental difference size-wise in people's heads across the globe. The evidence would suggest that only relatively small variations have been detected to date.

Do autists think in the same way as neuro-typicals? In Chris's case there is an aspect of his thought processes that is most certainly different from that of other people and might be said to illustrate that his brain is indeed wired up differently. It is in consideration of the words:

"What if?"

The whole world is full of what-ifs. They provide a way for an individual to be able to balance, reason, discuss, think and argue across any number of related perspectives before being prepared to offer a personal opinion or intended course of action. Historically these what-ifs have largely been absent from Chris's behaviour. Being disposed to a binary predilection, he would give a yes or no to almost any input or query delivered to him. These responses being primarily related to a choice between the two options rather than any evident reasoning being applied.

In those early days this was believed to be him giving a response simply because a response (any response) was what was wanted. The response was almost invariably "no", with only very rare examples of "don't know". This was thought to represent what might be a defence mechanism, signifying 'no' as in 'no action' with no change of status and no consequence to him as such. This is a bit of an over-simplification but hopefully the interpretation stands up to inspection.

This input and output performance has grown to be a more extensive consideration. His brain now seemingly interrogates the continuing and increasingly personal knowledge base inside his head before coming out with a response, albeit that this computation is a rapid one. The analogy drawn is that it is rather like having to trawl through the total contents of a car's operating manual before finding the page that might contain the information required.

He is getting better at looking at the index or contents list first but, again, this is work-in-progress. His personal research capabilities are extensive and responses continue to be very quick indeed.

This may also explain why, when faced with new software or a new computer game he usually studiously avoids reading the instruction manual and dives straight in to the game or software.

As long as knowledge and memories continue to be assimilated, the greater his knowledge base will be and the better he should continue to evolve in terms of interaction and responsiveness.

Dare one say he therefore becomes more intelligent the older he gets? That's an interesting premise. As the size of his head is now pretty well set, this extra and increasing knowledge based information has to be stored somewhere. Perhaps in due course his first-class neural pathways will become clogged by second-class post. Perhaps not. In any event it has to be said that his ROM (Read Only Memory) is well-established but his RAM (Random Access Memory) is expanding. He has a real living interface.

Chris's software – particularly his syntax interface

As far as the reference to syntax is concerned, he has no association with nor appreciation of sin so under other circumstances this account could be understood to be settled in full, i.e. tax paid. If this attempt at humour is obscure, then delay no more upon the matter and continue with the narrative regardless.

"… *but no syntax errors*" was a phrase coined by Chris over the dinner table one day.

He was voicing this in relation to past, sometimes exasperating, experiences with his computer-related activities. Whilst he is very logical in himself with his undergraduate degree module studies and their content, his logic apparently does not always coincide with the very exacting way in which computers need to be told precisely what to do.

There is 'English' grammar but this does not always equate

with the requirements of 'computer' grammar which uses various languages to express data in a way that computers can understand and process. Each such language has specific convention requirements. For example, the PHP language will not allow variable names to begin with a number while ending a line of code with a colon instead of a semicolon in the C++ programming language, is an invalid character and causes a syntax error.

Syntax errors mean the program cannot understand commands based on the programming language rules. In programming, syntax refers to command arrangements akin to the rules of grammar and spelling.

When entry errors are made such as incorrect or invalid numbers, words, punctuation or equations, even by missing an opening or closing bracket, a computer often fails to understand what is intended and will therefore not run the program. A syntax error is basically a grammatical mistake made in communicating with a computer and the frustration, particularly from Chris's point of view, lies with the need to effectively resolve each and every such case of reported syntax error before achieving satisfactory computer program responses. If all is clear to the computer programmer and to the computer itself, then progress may be made and the program run to a conclusion.

Resolution of syntax errors is a debugging and testing exercise which may or may not require the use of established manual debugging procedures, or even conventionally available software to assist in the analysis. Linguistic, unrecognizable or improper format bugs may be easier to resolve since they are more apparent when viewed on a computer monitor screen. Here endeth the lesson.

Chris prefers to limit his direct involvement with computer coding to the minimum extent necessary to cope with the needs of his studies.

His powers of further developing levels of increased intuitive reasoning and interpretative capabilities are constantly evolving and adding to his knowledge base. This is in addition to the ability to act on, and interact with, these characteristics. In computer speak, it is as if he is in a go-to loop here but one which is good and constructive. This driver has some way to go but it is not at all fanciful that this may well turn out to be the power in his life.

He has now comfortably reached that stage in his life where he is well capable of realising and organising his own priorities by reason of choice.

CHAPTER FIFTEEN

A Most Unexpected Turn Of Events

Dear reader, are you prepared to follow to a dark, vulnerable, place? It will be a short diversion, but one where you will only feel the full effect if you are prepared to follow with an open mind and no defences in place. It is a place where nightmares can happen.

Imagine a sturdy knight of yesteryear, sheathed from head to toe in heavy armour, a thick and heavy shield on one arm and a sword held within its scabbard to the side. Our knight is riding, galloping at pace across a narrow bridge, under pressure, under stress because he is intent on making swift progress. His horse is fit enough for the battle but at the end of the day a horse is only a horse.

At full speed and desperate to continue onwards, there is a stumble. Horse and rider are thrown into the deep but slow flowing river with the knight still atop the horse. In that instant, all forward momentum is lost and there is now only a slow descent, astride a horse with legs still moving as if to maintain progress, but to no avail. Air bubbles escape from the horse, rider and vestments rising freely to the surface, but horse and rider continue their slow, inevitable, descent.

Down, down, how far to go? How soon a feeling of total loss? How soon the feeling of unremitting deeper and deeper darkness and the feeling of impending doom as the light fades from above? There is nothing that can change this situation. The worst of dreams, the ultimate of nightmares.

This situation invites a primordial scream, frustration, terror and pure fear.

Is this not akin to the feelings of an autist seemingly alone in a world where he cannot make himself understood, where communication seems impossible and there appears to be no future and nobody to help him with the overbearing burden he cannot relinquish?

In such circumstances, how will an individual autist escape from such a situation...and indeed, can he? Well, that is surely down to his circumstances and some are more easily manageable than others. Remember, no two autists are the same.

The advancement for most autists from these sorts of depths involves trust, a helping hand, support, a feel, a touch, a word, compassion, empathy, encouragement, guidance, along with determination, bloody-mindedness, discipline, the input of tenderness, teaching, learning, enlightenment, understanding, responsiveness...the list goes on. What to hold on to and draw near and what to discard? Who to trust and believe and who to be wary of? Negatives and positives.

Where to start is another consideration. Peel back the layers of the onion until the bare truth of the situation is clear. Begin building, don't stop, make steps, record progress, learn lessons, deliver reasoning, offer choices, propose solutions, discuss, analyse, interact, persevere, inquire, question, resolve.

Discard that utmost negative of thoughts, absolute fear, by placing fear and all those thoughts of bad dreams into a big box trunk. Lock it with the heaviest padlock imaginable and throw it hard to the back of the mind, so far back that whilst knowledge of it still exists, the precise location becomes mired in the mists of time.

Recognition

Anxieties are a slightly different matter for Chris to cope with, but which over the years, he has been better able to vocalise, evaluate and elucidate. This goes along with his greater level of understanding of a response to him and the ability to offer a response or reaction in return. For irresolvable, bad or conflicting thoughts he has accepted the philosophy of...

"Go. You are not part of my life, my memories, my needs or interests. Now, simply go!"

He has the strength and ability to see this through.

Fear in all its guises is something everyone comes up against and has to learn to cope with and, where possible, resolve one way or another. Fear of the unknown is surely the greatest challenge of all. How does one deal with it? For Chris there was the situation where, in earlier days, circumstances which he might have identified and categorised as fearful would have been less capable of being resolved by him simply due to lack of knowledge and underdeveloped powers of reasoning at that stage. Self-evidently, as time has gone on, he has become more adjusted to, and comfortable with, categorising and classifying such thoughts in a manageable way due in no small measure to his own developing abilities and self-help.

"You need to think outside the box."

This is a terrible and often over-used phrase. The point here is one of recognition and surely the art is to recognise if you need to be inside or outside the box in relation to a specific set of circumstances. Recognition has grown in Chris just as he himself has grown and developed, giving him yet another arrow in his burgeoning quiver of armaments against the dark arts. Steady on there, steady on!

Management

In 2016 and 2017 he was more than ever concerned with managing his dark, negative thoughts. Dad and Mum kept emphasising that it was entirely natural to have negative as well as positive thoughts. This is reminiscent of the constant battle between the concepts of good and evil in the wider world.

It is real progress that by now he at least recognises this eternal conflict. He is quite adamant that he would not give in to actually doing wrong or bad things and, in time, clarification may become apparent as to what he actually classifies as wrong or evil deeds and, more importantly…why?

There is a large degree of sympathy here for Chris when the internet and the worldwide web is but a click away and full of good things, bad things, questionable things and things that are just plain evil by any stretch of the imagination. Further food for thought for him in that lifelong struggle of separating good from evil. A matter of personal judgement at the end of the day.

Historically, surprises (and here is meant good ones rather than bad), had an unfortunate impact on his demeanour because he did not like them much, if at all, and generally the bigger the surprise, the bigger the reaction. At worst he would take an opposing reaction to the hoped for enthusiastic and excited response on the revelation of the surprise. At best, he might merely offer a muffled endorsement. In those days he would have absolutely no background to draw on to satisfy his profound anxiety in such matters.

The consequence of these reactions has been re-visited with him many times over his development. These days, his attitude to any such surprise, be it large, small, urgent, or future planned, has graduated to the extent that he will now invariably invoke his standard phrase.

"Well that's a most unexpected turn of events." This accompanied by a wry smile.

He remains inquisitive about his world and the people and forces which impact on it, but will now accommodate change more openly.

In the words of the song.

"The darkest hour is just before dawn."

To return to the analogy of our sturdy knight, Chris was not believed to be so far down in the water as some autists might have been. As of now, he has raised himself from his own murky depths, dried himself off and achieved the status of offering himself as…

Available:

One-off: *Shiny Armoured Knight, prepared to tilt at dragons or windmills in equal measure*

As far as the family is concerned, whilst there were darker times in days of yore, like some of the situations Chris would have found himself subject to, there were no insurmountable blacks or whites…only management of shades of grey. As a family all are now, thanks be, living their lives in glorious Technicolour. Note from Dad – other colour formats are available.

CHAPTER SIXTEEN

I'm From Stardust – My Brother's From Dark Matter

There is no defence against a smile.

Chris, by the nature of his disposition, offers a calming influence, measured steps and an interest in all things and people he comes into contact with. He is an intriguing personality. His older brother has rather more experience of the world by dint of having been in it longer and has a heart of gold, usually worn on his sleeve, and long and strong steps. Well, he is the taller of the two after all. He has a committed loyalty to family, friends and acquaintances unless they have demonstrated that they are not worthy of that trust. So are they the same?...errr...no.

Older brother, Thomas, grew up in the *Jurassic Park* film era. He evolved with an overwhelming interest in dinosaurs and this description relates to the generic name of the whole panoply of prehistoric animals in the public domain. When one is a small child growing up, it is not uncommon for a particular pastime to catch the imagination. As to why and to what degree and to what benefit for someone like Thomas is again food for thought. Here was an all-consuming passion for him which as the years have passed remains more of a committed, but not exclusive, interest. He looks back on such times with real affection.

He went on to develop his Jurassic interest into the realms of the *Lord of the Rings* and *The Hobbit* films as progressively compiled and sent out on general release at the cinema.

He would delve into the background stories, taking an interest in director Peter Jackson, characters such as Gollum, Sean Bean as Boromir and his excellent death scene in *The Fellowship of the Ring*, character relationships, how certain scenes were filmed, continuity errors in the filming and more. He became almost word perfect in terms of the screenplay. The whole family has seen the films many times now.

This *Lord of the Rings'* interest led him in parallel to a system of interactive gaming called *Warhammer*. This and other game systems, such as 40k, involve competing as individuals or teams in model army game scenarios, moving hand-painted combatant models and armour around in battle on pre-prepared gaming tables with any amount of variable terrain.

One aspect of this gaming is the need for the players to paint their own armies, machinery and artillery they might wish to use in battle. This is a really big business.

Thomas used to run a *Warhammer* gaming club in a local scout hut. From *Warhammer*, interest spread to the Malifaux franchise which is essentially a development of *Warhammer*. Again, gaming is taken very seriously during combat but there is much fraternal respect away from the battlefield. There are all sorts of competitions and leagues and great kudos to be gained in producing the painted miniature models and armour to a high standard for battle.

This aspect of Thomas's life cannot pass without an acknowledgement of the very high standard of painting he has himself been able to achieve for his models, some of which are ridiculously small. It has to be said that it gives his parents much pride to know the high level of respect given by others in the genre to the quality of his painting and level of gaming ability.

If you will permit a small diversion, please visit his up to date Instagram site of Planetmithril for direct access to photographs of his latest painted models. The Facebook site of Tom Thorpe and even his Twitter page <Tom Thorpe@WyrdTom> show earlier developments of his craft. You are challenged not to find his photographs and abilities anything other than impressive.

Thomas lives, breathes, and largely contentedly, exists in the real world, though amongst his other hobbies he has a deep forensic interest in things that some might find daunting by virtue of the subject matter. This involves insensitive beasts and not necessarily live ones at that. This covers things like *The Walking Dead* on FOX TV, plus the magazines associated with the storyline(s), Zombies (any size, any shape, any genre), Simon Pegg's excellent Zombie film trilogy, horror flicks and his own earlier film making (viz: his Farnborough 6th Form 'Oscar' documentary film award). Creepy, but then why is he such a nice person with it? Don't know.

By comparison …

By inclination, Chris has altogether gentler interests such as Mario, Super Mario, like-minded electronic games and games characters. Bronies though are top of his list. He also has a firm belief in the goodness of all people and is so disappointed when he sees the sort of strife that makes the headlines in news bulletins.

He becomes concerned when he sees situations where there is conflict, discord or evident and wilful deceit used for unfair advantage. Talking and outlining reasoning, along with explanations at home, helps to moderate, and where possible, reconcile such concerns.

Both brothers give great attention and application to their

hobbies and interests but not to the extent that they let these things truly govern their lives in the real world.

There was one particular occasion in February 2017 when Thomas had popped back home for something to eat after work. Conversation was bouncing around the dinner table and Chris was in particularly effusive form. Sanguine brother, who was concentrating more upon the effort expended in reducing the contents of his dinner plate, gave limited input to the proceedings preferring to acknowledge responses by a taciturn frown or a tilt of the head.

Chris continued with his train of thought.

"I'm from stardust...my brother's from dark matter."

A 'gesture' was offered by way of a considered response, and all gave in to hearty laughter.

CHAPTER SEVENTEEN

Hello Bro!

Brothers are strange things.

As individuals, they are the product of an esoteric mixture of chemicals formed in the heat of battle, usually to appear nine months hence, bright-eyed, expectant and demanding. Circumstances, care, individuality, personal characteristics, along with all the other variables one can think of contribute to the building process.

And then along comes another one.

Same recipe:	No (although the implements were the same).
Same characteristics:	No (but both certainly have character).
Same personality:	No (not on your Nellie).

As brothers, there is an initial status of natural superiority based on age. That superiority might change over the years of course because, although the ingredients may be the same, the menu may not necessarily compute.

Do they grow up together or apart? Do they share? Do they interact? Are they each challenging? In the case of this family, they played together and laughed together. Challenging, well, yes of course.

When Chris was five years old his brother was having a problem with one of the electronic games bought for him. At an early stage of the game there was a scene where a number of prehistoric monsters were laid out on rocks. The inference was that clicking on one or another of these would reveal the next scene and enable progress through the game. After repeated attempts, Thomas was becoming more and more frustrated at being unable to clear this hurdle. Particularly so as he was totally dotty about dinosaurs in general and *Jurassic Park* in particular.

Mum was called in to clean the disc, to no avail, she offered sympathy and observed that the instruction manual appeared to offer no help either.

"There must be something wrong with the disc. I'll take it back for a replacement tomorrow."

Chris heard the hiatus and ventured, under the sufferance of his older brother, into the vault that was Thomas's bedroom. He did not know anything about the game, it was a new one after all, and made no comment. He merely picked up the mouse and clicked directly onto an innocuous area of rock face. Bingo! Much chagrin was exhibited on the part of older brother as the next scene was revealed, but at least he could now progress his game.

Playing together is such an important part of growing up. Learning about each other, interacting and competing with each other, relationships with the adults who provided the roof over their heads, money to do things with and food to be able to grow up. All this along with no little affection of brother for brother it has to be said.

Both boys grew individually of course. One physically more than the other, but at six foot seven inches against six foot one, who's going to argue? The prime outcome has been a deep affection between them, trust, understanding and lots of laughter.

Children's birthday parties were slightly different for the boys. Chris would be there for his, but his participation was largely nominal in nature and conventionally insular, with limited integration and usually with an adhesive hand hold on his beloved games console. Older brother was rather more interactive and excitable for his own birthday party events. The post-party chaos always seemed to require the same effort to clean up after in both cases. Mothers are usually good at this.

Excursions as a family have been touched on earlier, but the trip to Battle Abbey in Battle, and then along to Hastings comes to mind. Going down the route of the smuggling caves from the castle was great fun for the boys and then to exit right in the middle of town was a complete surprise for both of them. Rack and pinion rides in cabins up the cliff face with its steep gradient at Hastings and, on another occasion, at West Cliff, Bournemouth, caught Chris's interest.

More games…more understanding

The family has a reasonably sized garden and the boys had great fun in the inflatable paddling pool. The garden used to have a modest slope from one corner at the top across and down to the bottom corner which came in handy when the roll of plastic sheeting was laid along the route.

Water added to this makeshift slide meant that young ones were able to slide down in various ways with great amusement. A spot of washing-up liquid added to the slide increased the velocity profile significantly and the vocal volume of the participants substantially.

Thomas on occasion took surreptitious custody of the squeezy bottle of washing-up liquid. He would be rather less circumspect than his mother with the contents. These sessions usually took place during periods of sunny weather and when the boys were done, they would present themselves for inspection, looking like two mischievous yet triumphant chimney-sweep urchins.

"Ohhhhh nooo! Wait right there. Do not move!"

They had to be kept clear of the pool and would be subjected to a summary drenching with the hose pipe, up, down, round and round before scampering off for a shower. Great fun.

To be comfortable in your own skin

That's quite a target. Over the very long time of their joint development Thomas was to have a real impact on Chris's understanding of game playing and what Chris's reactions would lead to.

Chris's attitude towards games and gaming in the early days was that whenever he was in competition, be it one-to-one or indeed, group or paired conflict, he would become upset at losing, irrespective of the nature of the game. Even in board games or card games round the dining table with the family, he would dislike losing.

Did he take losing as an excuse to be upset with his competitor or competitors? No. He never gave any impression of wanting to physically beat the living daylights out of any victor. It was as if he was so sure of the outcome of the puzzle or game that he could not actually understand that someone might be able to do it better or quicker. In simplistic terms, based on his notable adding-up and subtraction capabilities, he simply could not accept that he had got it wrong or had made a mistake or that he was just plain unlucky. At that time he would have had little understanding of the ethereal concept of luck. That might explain a lot.

To him there was only right or wrong, black or white, no in-between, no middle ground and in his own mind the actual validity of the 'no' was evidently inconceivable. He was sometimes quite upset with himself on such occasions until gentle words brought him round to his regular demeanour.

Trying to explain to him that sometimes the matter of making a choice is more than just selecting between two specific options, Mum asked:

"Chris, what do you get if you put black and white together?"

His rapid response was not 'grey', it was:

"A checkerboard."

When then asked what happened if one *mixed* black and white, his response was:

"Grey."

Go figure.

The family was, of course, aware of his games-related behaviour. Over a period of time there was to be a measure of success in reiterating how games are played and how to react at the end of the game, win, lose or draw.

At home, as much time as was needed could be spent supporting him and mollifying his responses. Snakes and Ladders, Ludo, Pass the Pig, plus one momentous, though not altogether successful, game of Monopoly, were the sort of games played as a family foursome around the table. Over time and by means of gentle persuasion, Chris was able to accept all possible outcomes.

Freemantles also worked on this at length and, with the comprehension the staff were able to instil, this part of his make-up evolved quite successfully. Once he learnt something and accepted it, he logged it in his brain and did not forget it, nor would he regress. More and more he began to actively seek out game challenges, being determined to congratulate or commiserate with his opponent(s) as either condition might warrant at the end of the game.

. He has now developed a real understanding of fair play which has spread to other aspects of his general outlook. So, between school and home he was now armed with a set of reactions he could transpose into real life situations.

All these and more are reasons why Chris is so pleased to see his brother whenever he can and he will invariably greet him loudly.

"Hello Bro!"

Brotherly love

When Thomas was about five years old he and his younger brother developed an interest in steam trains. They happily shared the building of, and playing with, those wooden block train sets popular at the time.

Early one weekend morning, Thomas hove into view in the parental bedroom, just before they planned to rise for the day.

"I've made some train tracks for Chris."

"Oh, that's nice."

"They're green," continued Thomas.

Quizzical glances were shared and, though unspoken, there was that joint parental sense of foreboding and trepidation that relations with small children can sometimes engender.

"I wonder what that's all about?" was followed by provision of dressing gowns and an appropriately swift descent of the stairs.

The evidence was clear.

The colour of the lounge carpet was cream. Well, it used to be. Now it was what might best be described as 'cream plus'.

Thomas had drawn a straight length of track the full nearly nineteen-feet length of the lounge carpet. That's about 5.75 metres to more modern folk. He obviously had time on his hands, because he had then embellished this provision with copious additional train tracks of variable geometry. Some of these tracks would have required rather sharp navigation on the part of any train driver, but no matter, coverage was extensive and reminiscent of a chaotic and hastily re-planned Clapham Junction layout.

The marker pen used for this activity was green, which rather stretched the imagination, but nonetheless the distinct impression was that completion of the exercise had coincided with depletion of the available ink from the pen.

The further observation to be made here is that the ink from the pen was indelible.

Parental reaction? Well, take your pick. However, be assured that no smiting was involved.

The contrite miscreant was set to work with a bowl of water, detergent, scrubbing brush and the like. All to no avail, but the message had been duly served and received.

The insurance assessor looked at Mum in the way that only one who has had kids himself could do.

"Mrs Thorpe – this is an insurance claim."

Party time

Music plays a significant part in most people's memories, impacting relationships, goals, achievements, disappointments, grief, tragedy, rewards and outright unadulterated joy.

Music sets the tone. It can be loud, soft, soulful, stirring, strident or reflective but surely the common thread is one of emotion.

So many stories, good and bad, have been set to musical accompaniment. So many experiences able to be shared within any group of people or mused on individually. Dad and Mum are no different and in their own approach to music have their own favourites and memory markers.

An early favourite was **AIWITATIBATLY** which arose out of

Dad's musings in the bath one time in that early period when they were still getting to know one another. Yes, it was a long time ago. Yes, he was on his own at the time. **AIWITATIBATLY** was a phrase shared between them on many occasions. It was something of a trigger word between them and still brings a smile to the face when the song comes on the radio.

The family were determined to push the boat out to mark a celebration of the number 111 by organising a fancy dress party under that banner. The party was also to serve as a charity function to raise money for Help For Heroes. There were to be some 100 guests at a popular local facility permanently set up as a mock baronial hall and much in demand for that very reason. The place appealed to their sense of humour.

The fancy dress idea worked really well. Lots of friends had gone to great trouble to help make the event a success. The evening started well and got better the longer things went on – excellent! Mum had started out as Audrey Hepburn, complete with hair, sunglasses and cigarette holder and halfway through the evening was to morph into a southern belle (or bar room floosy – take your pick), in a dramatic red, flouncy, hooped, full-length dress (think *Gone With The Wind*), to make her reappearance to the tune of Jolene played by the DJ. Dad was Mr Pickwick with top hat, cane and boots.

Thomas was Captain Jack Harkness (aka John Barrowman) from *Doctor Who*, circa 2005, complete with superb ankle-length style pseudo RAF greatcoat. Chris was all dressed up as Mario, the Italian plumber from the video games. Great fun was had by all.

So how do you mark the support given to the family cause of the youngest son by one particular member of the family, a very important young man? Someone who had to grow up quicker than his years by virtue of his brother's condition. Someone who had been steadfast and unstinting in his support and consistently promised serious ill-will to anyone causing strife to his brother.

Someone who had declared his intention to be fully responsible for his brother in the years to come for as long as may be required and to whatever level necessary. The best way is in front of witnesses – lots of 'em.

To clarify the reasoning behind the number 111 associated with the party, well, a certain member of the family had reached a 'significant age', he and his dear 'significant other' had achieved a twenty-fifth wedding anniversary and Chris was twenty-one. You do the math.

What the heck does **AIWITATIBATLY** mean? Well, it is a ballad by The Hollies entitled…**All I Want Is The Air That I Breathe – And To Love You**. Lovely song.

Towards the end of this lively and successful party, Mum got up and made a dedication for a particular record to be played… especially for Thomas. Another Hollies song…

He 'Ain't Heavy – He's My Brother!

Big brother speaks

Some potted thoughts distilled from big brother about his younger brother and more or less in his own words would be most appropriate here. However, for reasons best kept for the future, for the moment the timing is not quite right nor is the time available to feature the extensive detail that he would want to contribute about his own beloved brother Chris. Hold that thought.

CHAPTER EIGHTEEN

Brohoof

The family foursome, plus Thomas's girlfriend at the time travelled up to London by train for the day, in celebration of Thomas's birthday.

They walked across Waterloo Bridge on that lovely sunny summer's day, turning around on approaching the north bank of the Thames to view The Shard. They continued up through Charing Cross railway station to find a suitable stop for refreshments. Waterstone's book shop was next on the list.

The target for the younger members of the party was the Forbidden Planet Megastore in Shaftsbury Avenue, so named after the science fiction film of the same name. The film had scared Dad witless at the time when he saw it as a youngster in 1956 (heavens that was a long time ago!) and that wasn't just due to Robby the Robot either. There was a successful London stage production of the same name much, much, later which Dad and Mum went to see with friends. This franchise covers just about every aspect of cult science fiction memorabilia, models, magazines and books imaginable. This was a must-do stop in the day's itinerary. Everyone left the store heavily laden.

Shortly afterwards Dad, Mum and Chris were minding the many purchases whilst waiting outside the HMV store in Oxford

Street for the other two to finish shopping inside. Then, bold as brass, a guy who must have been in his 30s walked right up to Chris in the street.

"Brohoof!" he announced and presented a right-handed knuckle by way of salutation.

This was responded to without hesitation by Chris in similar fashion with their knuckles gently meeting. There was no further conversation and the man went on his way, still a complete stranger.

What could all that have been about? This guy was wearing a stiff-brimmed style of boater hat but there appeared no commonality or mutuality to draw on although, wait a minute, he was wearing a Brony T shirt and so was Chris. Enough said. It wasn't knuckles meeting, but hooves. This all came from *My Little Pony*, not the series beloved of small girls but the progression of it, now a significant cult amongst young men especially in the USA.

Chris is a most committed Brony and has many and various plush models of each of the pony characters in his bedroom, as if surrounding himself with a loyal, trusty, honourable and moral group of good friends. Just what, pray, could be wrong with that then?

There are six main (or mane) named character ponies each representing a specific attribute:

Twilight Sparkle – Magic
Rarity – Generosity
Pinkie Pie – Laughter
Applejack – Honesty
Rainbow Dash – Loyalty
Fluttershy – Kindness

A seventh but less prominently featured pony is Sunset Shimmer, representing Empathy.

Bronies are a very big thing in American colleges today. Avoiding the temptation for gentle cynicism at this stage, the interest here is that such characteristics have wide appeal and represent an idealistic innocence. Many quite mature people do also take on the mantle of being a Brony and live out their lives substantially committed to the precepts of Bronyhood.

There are many books, magazines, videos, on-line communications and whole conventions related to these gentle life-affirming morality stories. Simple but sincere.

What does Chris get out of the Bronies? Well they give him a group of friends that he can directly interact with on his own ground rules. Having a friend or acquaintance on purely human terms involves a degree of compromise which may or may not prove problematic to him. Anyway – it is good to have friends. The Brony byword is Friendship Is Magic.

The thought occurs that this is rather like James Stewart's inseparable rabbit friend in the film *Harvey*, but is not so in terms of Chris and his demeanour. Harvey appears to fulfil a singular purpose and to all intents and purposes is actually invisible. Bronies offer a whole range of interactions and are most certainly visible. The interaction here for Chris is from a different perspective because Bronies reoccur in his activities as and when he wishes, they are not welded to him.

Bronies have given Chris an extended interest in fiction books. To anyone else this might appear a matter of little regard, but to the family this represents a humungous step forward for Chris. To see him at the age of twenty-four devouring a Brony story in hardback book form of the order of 100-plus pages with no illustrations, drawings or photographs, just text, is no more and no less than a real joy. This is a meaningful progression from his earlier Yu-Gi-Oh, Manga and Simpsons comics which, though still popular with him, are demonstrably no longer the limit of his ambition.

CHAPTER NINETEEN

The Autistic Gameworm

Chris has been electronic gaming for many years and in terms of portable and home based consoles he has known and loved, there have been more than you can poke a stick at. Try some of these for example:

PC (obviously)	Nintendo DS X	Nintendo Wii	Microsoft XBox
Gameboy	Nintendo 3DS	Nintendo Wii U	Microsoft Xbox 360
Gameboy Colour	Nintendo DS Lite	Nintendo Switch	Gamecube
Gameboy Advance	Nintendo DS1	PlayStation One	TV Joyboy
Gameboy Advance SP	Nintendo DS1 XL	PlayStation Two	Nes
Nintendo 64	Nintendo New 3DS	PlayStation Three	New 2DS XL
Nintendo DS	Nintendo 3DS XL	PlayStation Four	

These days the graphics on racing games are really impressive and when Chris takes his mates Mario and Luigi, those inveterate Italian plumbers, out for a kart race run on a large-size screen, much fun ensues.

This chapter contains detailed references regarding the diverse worlds of *Pokémon, Digimon, Yu-Gi-Oh* and *Anime*. Their origins, development, content, characters, game content and impact are relevant here without apology because they are very important to Chris. This is where Chris spends much of his free time – possibly too much time. Be assured that by the time you approach the subject of the Boileroom here, however, you may be on safer ground.

Thomas had gained exposure to the gaming franchise of *Pokémon* in the early days of its deployment. *Pokémon* – pocket monsters – originated in Japan and relates to a points-based system of a whole range of power battles between contestants. Games are played for fun and kudos.

The franchise grew rapidly. It is a card-playing game where battles are fought between contestants holding a range of playing cards in their possession. Each card features a particular character with an assigned set of characteristics and attack/defence properties. Cards can be bought in the shops as individual cards or packs of cards and some of these cost considerably more than others due to their rarity value.

There is a strong secondary market in these trading cards so players can develop their set of cards for optimum potency. The possibilities are endless. The franchise has since expanded to the internet and games consoles, allowing endless challenges at home and abroad. The principle behind the game is to allow the basic characters to evolve to the next, higher level of existence, repeat this ad infinitum, and defeat the opponents' *Pokémon* characters in battle.

Chris picked up on *Pokémon* not long after Thomas and they

enjoyed many pitched battles across the dining room table. Chris's first favourite character was Pikachu. This is a short, chubby, cuddly rodent *Pokémon* covered in yellow fur with two horizontal brown stripes on its back. It has a small mouth and long, pointed ears with black tips and is classified as one of the 'electric' *Pokémon*.

'Electric' *Pokémon*, with the ability to fire electric bolts, are relatively few in number. Many other characters exist within the range of *Pokémon* categories such as 'normal', 'ice', 'fire', 'fighting', 'bug', 'dark', 'psychic', 'water', 'rock', 'steel', 'poison', 'ground', 'ghost', 'fairy', 'grass', 'flying', 'dragon'. Each *Pokémon* has different battle, power, attack and defence characteristics. Should you have need of details regarding the apparently infinite range of battle scenarios, it would be as well to gain the confidence of one or more young aficionados for enlightenment. However, by such means, you may have to be prepared to submit to many years of detailed study!

Chris's other favourite characters are Gallade, a newer character, and, currently vying with Pikachu to be his selected favourite, Zekrom and Primarina.

Initially there were 150 characters associated with the franchise, now it appears there are some 800+. ("And counting," says Chris.)

Moving on from the odd foray into the world of comics, *Pokémon* now gave him the first real impetus to develop an interest in fiction as a whole. He even exposed his parents to the *Pokémon* feature film at the cinema. Mum was to see the film with him again and, somewhat worryingly, said she understood more about it the second time around.

Digimon – digital monsters – was the American equivalent of *Pokémon* and designed to be in direct competition. The Japanese won this battle and *Digimon* did not really take off to the same degree. Mum was to attend the *Digimon* film with the boys. It was dire. There were very few people in the cinema and she, for one, came out at the end dazed, severely unimpressed and knowing less about the whole subject at the end than she did at the beginning. But at least Chris had been supported although he took little further interest in the *Digimon* franchise. Dad appears to have got off scot-free here.

"No change there then," says Mum.

Yu-Gi-Oh followed *Pokémon* into the family home. It is another card-based gaming system originating in Japan. Thomas started with it but his interest lapsed after a time. *Yu-Gi-Oh* attracts a slightly higher age group than *Pokémon*, being rather more complex in nature and structure. Chris finds it great fun interacting with the Manga characters, who are highly stylised and distinctive action figures involved in detailed scenarios and stories.

Chris has a very wide collection of *Yu-Gi-Oh* cards, and once a fortnight used to go to a gaming session in Camberley on a Saturday. He has long since gained the knowledge and pleasure of simply competing. At collection time from the shop Dad would ask of Chris how he got on.

"Came second. Won one – lost two," was the almost regular response.

He would usually be in possession of one or more new packs of gaming cards awarded as prizes during the day, and sometimes report that he had actually come first. He really enjoyed those competition days.

He would buy the *Yu-Gi-Oh* / Manga comic books, as and when shopping trips loomed. He was often to be seen engrossed, quite content to follow the stories all the way through. This was no mean feat as the books, being Japanese, are read from back to front! Other regular comic purchases followed. This was a significant leap forward for him.

Chris's avid interest and deep involvement in the world of *Pokémon* and *Yu-Gi-Oh* continues unabated. He asked if he could go to the *Anime and Gaming Convention* in London. This was to be a three-day summer event at the London Metropolitan University,

166-220 Holloway Road, near to Highbury and Islington tube station.

It was clearly inappropriate for him to travel all that way and back on his own even if he had been able to accommodate and follow the route. At that point Thomas jumped in.

"I'll take him if you like."

With confidence and trust in older son's capabilities, but some lingering parental concerns for the whole venture, permission was granted and a one-day visit planned. It would be an adventure for both of them.

Anime (from Japan) is an ever-expanding, highly stylised, science fiction based set of fantasy-themed fiction stories. Originally hand drawn, but now more and more produced by computer animation, the main features of the genre are the striking visual impact and colourful graphics. The characters themselves are designed to be visually arresting, vibrant, generally of human form and proportions (give or take), but with overly large and exaggerated eyes, imposing hairstyles and brightly coloured clothing. The main sub-genre description covers the action-based Manga comics and novels.

Anime covers a very wide range of interest, with different stories appealing to different age ranges covering children, boys and girls, adolescents and adults. It cannot be denied, however, that, by virtue of the open licensing philosophy, the adult stories available on the internet sometimes veer into what can only be described as truly adult themes. Censorship has to be a matter of personal judgement at this end of the market but it should not detract in any way from the wide, attractive, and worthy content proliferating at the proper and very acceptable end.

Exposure to the full extent of *Anime* offers a substantial degree of sensory overload in both auditory and visual terms. Chris appears to be able to cope quite well with this.

Pokémon and *Yu-Gi-Oh* come under the broad heading of *Anime*.

They do, however, have a life and evolution of their own with their distinct division of interest catered for within the wide range of activities, presentations and games available at the Convention. Chris wanted to play *Pokémon* and *Yu-Gi-Oh*. Anything else would be a bonus at this popular and extremely well-attended event.

The boys returned home much the better for the expedition and had enjoyed the day very much. Fortunately the transport arrangements had been satisfactory all round. Time for dinner and bed.

Chris, suitably enthused, wanted to go the following year. Unfortunately Thomas would not be available as chaperone this time, so Dad and Mum duly obliged. The exposure to that sensory overload proved all too real for them. At least it was a nice warm sunny day and there was a bar there.

The Boileroom

With the demise of his fortnightly Saturday *Yu-Gi-Oh* club, Chris was to have to think about moving further afield for his regular gaming fix. The Boileroom in Guildford hosts a monthly Games Lounge – Retro Gaming Club on Saturday afternoons. So, ok, it is a rather mature building with associated lumps and bumps but it serves its purpose well enough.

The Boileroom is described as a creative Arts and Music & Bar events venue founded by an 'independent collective'. Within this suitably darkened interior, Chris battles on the existing set-up machines. He reports that he regularly sees action on *Pokémon Stadium, Mario Kart 64, Super Smash Bros, Sonic the Hedgehog 3, Super Mario World, Gradius 3* and *Mario Party 2*. Surely quite enough entertainment to be had there. He continues his *Yu-Gi-Oh* battles online and elsewhere.

This Retro Gaming Club was to have further relevance to him as Dara O'Briain was hosting a rumbustious retro gaming programme on TV, Channel Dave, called *Go 8 Bit*. This was a television game show based on two teams battling in on-screen retro games like *Crash Bandicoot, Sonic The Hedgehog 2, Goat Simulator, Overcooked* and more. The show, described as a 'Consoles Meets Comedy – Panel Show', had been developed from the Edinburgh Fringe. Surely that says it all really.

For Chris, this was right up his street and a great bolt-on to his deep interest in the Saturday retro gaming club at the Boileroom.

He enjoyed *Go 8 Bit* hugely and, on the basis that it appeared to appeal to the uninhibited and unscripted side of his nature, his consequential unrestrained exuberance and enjoyment was entertainment in itself. This could be a great 'reveal' to any others within range. The show was frenetic and he made a lot of noise watching it.

As far as electronic gaming is concerned, he will avoid the *Grand Theft Auto* franchise, on the basis of it being too violent for him. Remember, he has a side to him that takes the stories and graphics as being more literal than others might do. He is actually not such a fan of shoot-'em-up games but will still give his older brother a real challenge when so gaming.

Thomas suffers no such inhibitions and is no slouch at all in shoot-'em-up games himself, being particularly inclined towards zombie-featured games. Again, that is a whole separate story in its own right. He and Thomas do share an interest in motor and kart racing games.

The parents were intrigued as to why Chris would on occasion be talking into his hand-held electronic games console in his room and indeed sometimes when he was out on the hoof. How he knew what to do was a mystery, but entirely self-taught, he had found out how to contact literally anyone in the world on his console, talk to them by such means and make combat, playing across a whole variety of games. He found it particularly interesting to battle with people in Japan.

What was being heard were conversations in real-time between Chris in good old England and someone in Japan, through the audio facility on the console, discussing their game and the outcome of it. He even learnt some Japanese words that way. Definitely intriguing. Dad and Mum had not explained or suggested how this could be done because, quite simply, they had not the foggiest idea how to do it, yet he did it himself. Clever bunny.

A number of other things about his computer activities fascinated his parents. Chris loved the short You Tube video clips and home-made cartoons uploaded onto the internet. So much so, he had decided to have a go himself. Several times he sought assurance that what he was doing was acceptable in terms of copyright because he was very concerned that everything should be legal and above-board.

Satisfaction was provided. If he utilised some copy from the web in what he produced that would not be a problem. The proviso was that he should not intend to sell it on the web himself in its modified form nor attempt to pass off any inserted material as being his own work. Since he did not intend to make money out of his production(s), he would just need to acknowledge the origin of the original piece of work, then he was clear to go ahead and make his own clips without fear of censure.

These clips are described as You Tube Poops. There are several forms of these clips produced by Chris including edited and superimposed artwork on existing cartoons, video gaming features and compilations of gaming reviews. He has produced over 100 of these Poops most of which are of relatively short duration. It has to be said that one of his Poops has had over 200,000 views. What still blows parental minds away is that this is self-taught research, development and compilation work.

Chris has even got to the stage where he has designed his own gaming card as an entry in an international design competition. It is called Raimos – The Thundering Storm. Notably as big a brute as could be imagined. He did the original design which was then firmed up for him by the international company as one of the winning designs. He has had his copyright for this card properly registered. It will not make him rich, but at least it is a start.

Small little creatures

Back in the days when his involvement with *Pokémon* was just beginning to evolve, there was the small matter of Tamagotchi. As with almost everything else at the time, Tamagotchi was of Japanese origin. These small, hand held, electronic pods were digital creatures requiring care, attention and husbandry on the part of their carer, a single point of contact, in order to be able to live, develop and evolve through several generations in their digital world.

It was necessary to feed them with digital food on demand. Indolence, inattention or bad practice on the part of the carer towards a Tamagotchi in need would result in its summary electronic demise. Chris took on the mantle of due care and attention for some eight individuals at differing times and, by his efforts, extended most lives well into a span of several months.

This was a great learning opportunity for him, based upon the need for self-control. There was no form of external competition or supervision involved. He reported that he and his peers sometimes got into trouble at school because pod response times were not pre-set and carers had to cope with indiscriminate timings for action during the school day. Chris had picked up Tamagotchi when he was twelve years old and had great fun with them until the time came, some six years later, to move on, when other interests required greater need of his attention.

How many batteries have been bought in support of maintaining a power capability for all his games and consoles, apart from when being cabled up? Don't ask! A notable carbon footprint could be said to apply. Looking on the bright side, rechargeable capability has been the thing for some time now. But then there is the electricity bill. Don't look!

Mechanical man

His abilities with pinball machines are legendary. A game of Chris verses the machine. The sight of him controlling a multi-ball play machine, with a minimum of three balls going round at the same time but in differing directions, whilst holding distracting conversations with bystanders, is quite amazing. His many record scores could be posted here but probably would not be believed.

It is a mere matter of fact that the bowling alley in Camberley no longer has pinball machines on the premises. That could well be just a policy decision but the thought that they probably never made any money from Chris may have had something to do with it to some small degree.

Pinball machines have similarly disappeared from the 'Big Apple' activity and games complex in Woking. There is also the arcade complex on the beach front at Shanklin, Isle of Wight, which the family hopes to revisit to check for residual collateral, Chris-inflicted damage.

"He 'aint deaf, dumb or blind but the kid can sure play a mean Pin-Ball".

Cue music…**loud!**

Watch and learn

Chris was helping Mum with the crossword strategy picture game she had downloaded onto her Ipad. The individual pages of the software each gave a picture at the top and a completely blank section of crossword squares below. The object of the game was to complete the two, three or more crosswords, deducing the answers from interpretation of the contents of these pictures. Completing the first page successfully allowed passage to the next. Increasing levels of difficulty were available.

Picture Mum staring valiantly at the screen, word-blind, frustrated and irritated that the five-letter response she has got will not fit the four spaces available. Youngest son peers over the screen and donates a valid response in a trice.

"Chris, that's remarkable."

Watch and learn...again

On several occasions Chris has been seen manipulating the many screens of the university web link showing Dad, at speed, the aspects of the homework he is revising or preparing for submission.

"Chris, that's remarkable."

Amazing young man. Much has been seen...much has been learnt.

CHAPTER TWENTY

Unexpecticups – Burpicups

Chris is a parental puzzle wrapped in an enigma, cloaked in a conundrum.

Communication between people is a necessity of life. It is a way of passing on information, concerns and enquiries from one to another, in the hope of receiving reactions and responses in return. By such means, knowledge is shared and at the end of the day surely this adds a measure of change, if not actual improvement, to the way in which people live their lives. A laudable trait, no doubt about that.

People communicate in different ways but surely this starts with the need for the spoken word. In simplistic terms, children will usually learn by repetition, by encouraging repetition of individual instructions to them, plus the multiple sensory inputs given consciously or sub-consciously at the time. Inputs such as tone, volume, emphasis, eye contact, body language and the like, until the reaction becomes an automatic response on the part of the child.

Repetition, repetition, and yet more repetition, leading hopefully and ideally, to satisfactory interpretation.

Very young children will usually learn to make themselves understood by means of analysing a parental response to their own utterings, and learning how to modify their own means of communication and corresponding physical gestures accordingly.

Having then understood the meaning of individual words and simple phrases in a two-dimensional, 'stick and carrot', 'do and don't do' sense, what then of the wider issue of concept? One word which comes to mind and is often used with children is:

"Behave!"

Generally used as a single word instruction, admonishment or expression of exasperation without any other words of explanation. Even to a non-autist, this presents a challenge of comprehension and interpretation by the recipient in order to be able to comply.

The mechanism here is to ensure children are constantly spoken to, irrespective of their make-up. Chris is indeed a curiosity but by his very nature he is someone who has great curiosity and an apparently never ending thirst for information. He wants to know the way things are and the way in which they interrelate. So, whilst like others, he may have the desire for knowledge, this is rather more on the basis of the search for enlightenment than the use or misuse of power. This sounds very much like Yoda speaking. Interesting, this is.

The question then arises as to how an autistic child learns the spoken word if indeed they are able to. There are many and various weighty tomes of reference books and reading material available for study on this very matter, written by those with a professional or vested interest. Rightly or wrongly, no such detailed historical, retrospective study work has been undertaken to date by any third-party relevant to Chris's particular situation. The main principals, Dad and Mum, remain committed observers.

The over-arching parental concern, especially in earlier days, was to focus on the perception of his needs rather to the exclusion of all other matters. This meant that parental hands were rather full at the time in the discharge of such duties.

Chris was speaking and communicating well enough by and large, or so the family thought, in advance of his diagnosis of autism at the age of three and a half. So, accepting that he has been autistic since birth, how did he get on? Looking back to a time before his diagnosis, he was quite a reflective child. He was interested in toys and interaction with his mum in particular, naturally and rightly so. He would accommodate nearly all types of food offered for consumption. He was, however, a late talker and the current retrospective observation might be...

"Did he feel the need at the time?"

Autists generally have difficulty in recognising, understanding, interpreting and responding to body language. Regrettably, to some at the more extreme end of the autistic spectrum, this matter of body language remains a closed book. Chris does have a rudimentary understanding. Direct use of language and interpretation of sounds would have been important aspects of his early development. Fortunately, then as now, he would always have been talked to.

The ultimate irony regarding the matter of body language to an autist is that someone could be saying something quite unpleasant but, because they had a smile on their face whilst saying it, the import of the message could be seriously misinterpreted by the autist who would usually be unable to read or analyse the body language. This is a difficult skill for them to master.

Chris's brain has been likened to that of a computer hard drive. It is not at all fanciful to think that he might have developed his own use of language, having slowly recognised the need for it. It may well have been just like an English person learning French for the first time. Initially there is the grammar, then the rules, followed by the vocabulary.

Grammar and rules have a fairly well-established sense of logic in spite of the wonderful idiosyncrasies of the English language. They can be mastered, with hard work and commitment, by people like Chris to a good working level over a reasonably short time span. The separate matter of vocabulary, or those words which add colour to language, is not always logical but picked up by experience, example and observation over time, to be stored and then used when appropriate. This could well be said to apply to Chris.

Message sent: Yes...
Message received: Yes...
Message understood: Not sure.

The need for effective communication aligned with means, methods and consequences is an important and most necessary feature of our world. Some are better at this than others. Those within the broad scope of the autistic spectrum may find this particularly challenging.

Chris communicates with those he has to, those he wants to, and those he needs to, in order to resolve those things within his immediate compass. This concern covers those points over which he needs control in the short term and, increasingly now, over consideration of future needs which might arise. Other than within the family, he does not generally initiate discussion or share opinions just for the sake of it. He does though, contribute to and respond to, topics raised by others.

To achieve valid comprehension the intent should be to be honest, open, enquiring, clear, concise, and explicit. Otherwise there is a danger of misinterpretation. How people communicate properly is fraught with difficulty.

Truth, accuracy and avoidance of offence are important concerns. How best to achieve this when, as everyone is different, there are innumerable options and interpretations? Any reasoned response would require substantial analysis in order to cover all the options.

Face to face communication is the ideal situation. In business this is not always possible or convenient. In social and personal circumstances, the distance between the parties often renders this to be likewise impractical.

From the parental point of view it is entirely appropriate to avoid thoughts of deliberate dishonesty, deceit and argument being directed towards Chris. Whilst these aspects may well be sadly evident in life as a whole, such intent is as far removed from Chris's character as may be imagined. These are simply not part of his make-up and he should be excused from any consideration of intent to cause deliberate argument or to engender discord.

Chris will communicate with the best of intentions and without malice, cynicism, sly intent, or the desire to confuse and conquer. Such matters are divisive and, because that would not be what he would intend, as far as he is concerned matters of confrontation and argument are for others to contend with. They are simply not part of his identity.

Sometimes the truth can be an early casualty as far as communication is concerned but Chris will always offer and support the truth.

Within any written communication there lie two concerns, or risks. Taking the first point, what is sent by the originator may not always be interpreted by the recipient in the manner intended. For the second point, the nature of the message and/or information given and its relative importance may, for whatever reason, cause offence. Chris would not wish to cause offence and would, truly, be mortified if he thought any word or deed from him would do so.

Then as far as that first point is concerned, humour may be the first casualty, and this in turn may easily be the cause of unintended offence. Great care should be given to the intent of humour in the written word between people who are not very close friends or trusted acquaintances.

As far as the second point is concerned, it is possible that, for whatever reason, sooner or later something said or sent by him will inadvertently actually cause offence. This is an ever-present consideration in Chris's methods and means of communication. Hopefully this would be an unlikely event but if it should occur, it needs monitoring, mentoring and modification, if not, mollification. Dad and Mum stand by to intercede appropriately and they will endeavour to provide context in advance where possible.

The start of this particular section of the book gives Chris a 'not sure' rating. The understanding of ethereal concepts of opinion, comprehension, interpretation, consequence, management, judgement and delivery are, as ever, work-in-progress. It is clear though that like him, and with him, that understanding is growing and developing.

Comprehension...akin to communication

If Chris understands the question he will be able to give a valid response. This may be as an answer, a comment or a reaction depending upon his interpretation.

When younger it was problematic to involve Chris in a conversation because he would act, react, or just say yes or no when spoken to. Over time he was prepared to vocalise more and more to the extent that he would actually initiate the start of a conversation, thread, or topic. This is something others might take for granted but which for Chris represented marked progress and real development.

He was then exposed to the concept of context. He would, and does still, ask the meaning of a particular word. The response to him is the same each time.

"Put it into a phrase or sentence and then we can say."

Answers are logged and stored in his hard drive brain. His vocabulary is getting bigger and better, widening and developing.

At the age of twenty-five he has the ability and desire to hold his own in conversation over the dinner table, using an extensive range of vocabulary, including much longer words than before. The joy here is that more and more he is using intelligent, selected, vocabulary precisely in the right context.

He has developed his vocabulary to the extent that he is not averse to inventing his own words. 'Unexpecticups' and 'Burpicups' are two such examples tabled by him describing his reaction to involuntary responses to certain of his bodily functions when in company. Most people might just have said, "Pardon me," and carried on but because the nature of both functions may well be understood to be hiccups and burps respectively, then his inventions have validity. They are certainly humorous and are recycled by him as and when he thinks it appropriate. Whether they stand as suitable entries to the Oxford English Dictionary depends, one imagines, on a wider take-up of the words by the population at large. Just don't hold your breath for that to happen.

Chris's planetary sized brain has adopted the recently developed philosophy that there may well be more than one plane of existence and that there is actually more than one universe. The more he harks back to the concept, the more he finds the theory, and therefore the possibility of multiverses appealing. He has no fear of such a future, should it ever be proven. Talking of this briefly one day around the dinner table at home, there was talk of space travel in general and the current progress of a satellite launched some forty years ago which is now out of our solar system.

The conversation developed around the way in which

knowledge might be gained and shared in such an environment, out there, in space. Chris had a simple and, to him, a most appropriate premise here.

"Multiversities." Aargh!

Watch out for the *Oxford English Dictionary* circa 2318.

Chris is now very quick to come back with a good pun in conversation.

"Just like his Dad," mourns Mum.

It was always known that Chris's reactions were very fast but now there was ample evidence that he had the wit to back it up. To the mock, reconciled, reticence of Mum, Dad is indeed fond of the occasional pun.

"What's with the occasional? It's rather frequent; too frequent," offers Mum.

Around the dinner table Dad might pick out a word for a pun, drawn from the context of the topic of conversation. This will engender the sort of reaction from Chris that involves pursed lips, a dummy frown, eyes rolled round, hand clasped to his forehead and head slumped forward with the offer of a Homer-esque "D'oh!" An entertaining sight in its own right, but then he will quite often come straight back with a counter pun of his own. This can pass backwards and forwards between the two combatants for some time. The one thing comedians will stress about comedy is that to make a good gag you must have timing. Chris, sharp as a tack, qualifies.

CHAPTER TWENTY-ONE

We'll Just Have To Do It Again Then Won't We

One feature of Chris's condition is the extent to which he and others like him, are inclined towards certain repetitive actions, inbuilt, well-established and repetitive.

The boundaries of such actions may differ between different autists and can change as individuals develop over the years. They serve to mark a broad sense of routine and regularity, being something they have a measure of control over.

If there is some rationale regarding the degree of personal expression given out (i.e. output), what of all the input, those lessons learnt, life instructions, skill and activity concepts that need to be understood, accepted and acted upon when appropriate? How about the 'learning to cross the road' lesson? Simple? Possibly. Essential? You bet yer life.

Road crossing, a vital skill, has to be done safely, consistently, in full knowledge of the surrounding situation. How was the family to give Chris the ability to manage and monitor this activity, to the extent they could be confident he could be relied upon to do it safely on his own? The answer here was repetition, repetition, repetition. When did it start?

Darth Vader, from the *Star Wars* films, made his impact on the nation's consciousness some time ago. Darth had two personas. Well, three actually. Firstly, in the early films he was not a very nice person at all. Secondly, he had the gravelly, distinctive voice of James Earl Jones. Thirdly, his physical presence was represented by an actor called Dave Prowse who was a really big man in real life.

Some might remember a much, much, earlier incarnation of Dave Prowse as the Green Cross Code man on ITV television. The representation by today's standards was rather naïve, being a jollied-up, green-garbed, Father Christmas type of character but without the beard. His function was to teach children the conventional way to cross the road safely. These days these things are referred to as 'info-mercials'. Check out the voice-over on these ancient clips if you can sometime. It's rather like someone trying to sell soap powder.

Chris hovered behind Dad just as this piece was being written. He was on his way to collect yet another bag of salt and vinegar crisps from the garage. That Mr Lineker has a lot to answer for.

"How's the book going, Dad?"

"Very well thanks, Chris. Remember that you are going to get the chance to read some of it and put your own views and observations down when it's nearly finished."

Chris interrogated the monitor screen.

"What's Darth Vader got to do with it?"

Having then explained that this section of the book was in relation to how he, Chris, had been taught to cross the road, he seemed satisfied. Before retiring with his crisps he said, "Perhaps Darth Vader should now be saying come over to the green side."

"Chris, go away – quickly!"

Actions...and more actions

The family was on holiday in the Isle of Wight with accommodation on the beach front in Shanklin, on the east side of the island. Access to the sandy beach required care and awareness to cross the road in front of the hotel and progression down the short flight of steps to the beach.

After some time doing what people do on beaches, Dad and Mum settled down to relax in the deck chairs. Then came the challenge.

"Mum, I want to go to the toilet."

So here's the thing, does the mollycoddling continue or not? Now is as good a time as any, thinks Dad.

"Chris, you know what to do, don't you? Up the steps, stop, look right, look left, look both ways again and wait to see that the way is clear, then cross the road only when you are totally sure it is safe to do so. Remember to do the same on the way back."

Armed with these instructions he went on his way to the evident concern of his mother.

"Well, he's got to do it some time," was his father's attitude.

Happily there was no sound of screeching brakes, only the safe return of the prodigal to the beach in due course. He had learnt well.

The instructions had been installed, downloaded, and he had activated the programme by himself.

It is necessary to impress on people like Chris the importance of regular repetitive actions, required not only for health and wellbeing but, most importantly, safety. Practice makes perfect. That practice includes the conscious or subconscious aspect of Chris setting reference points when undertaking a particular action or during the course of a journey, as control points in his mind. Typically, when travelling somewhere he should set some markers such as a distinctive building, a monument, or set of traffic lights and where they would expect to be seen at a particular stage of the journey.

Dad's much earlier pseudo-orienteering efforts along these lines were conventionally based upon marking the location of notable public houses. This study has involved considerable research and many site inspections over the years.

Regular reminders serve to instil and establish protocols. Activities like teeth cleaning, toilet workings, personal hygiene and shaving, apply for the male of the species. Other markers can be set for additional things done on a regular basis whether they be for relatively mundane activities or more important ones. All Chris would then need to do would be to log in the required actions in his brain and set start times for the work.

The rather more problematic concern is what happens with regard to those more important activities, even just one-off events, which are not necessarily actioned daily or reasonably regularly? They may not even occur in the company of a family member, relative or carer. His memory is a good place to start by way of management, but Chris really does have to apply himself with a certain discipline to specifically record the dates of future appointments so he can try at least to accommodate planned events. It is the unplanned or irregular ones which give more food for thought.

Once a year is irregular enough here for one particular event. This one he looks forward to with relish.

He now takes complete control of the front door for All Hallows Eve activities (Halloween). He enjoys getting dressed up, who doesn't? One year as Darth Vader, other times as the *Phantom of the Opera* or Edvard Munch's *The Scream*. When the doorbell goes for the first time he hurtles downstairs for the first trick-or-treat encounter.

Leaving a plentiful supply of sweets in Chris's care, the adults have already retired to the lounge for the hour or so of entertainment. It is rather like listening to the radio for that amount of time. Chris is a closet thespian who throws himself into his role for the night with great abandon. Demonic gestures and an inventive script are on offer every time there is a call to be answered. There have been many enjoyable encounters, especially with larger parties. A peek through the curtains will reveal who calls on such dark nights.

Towards the end of the year

It is not long then before the onset of the pantomime season. The family will normally go to the Victoria Theatre in Woking. Particularly good shows in the past have been where Henry Winkler (The Fonz) was brilliant in *Peter Pan* (don't really understand or know why that's a panto but never mind), and the trio of John Inman, Lionel Blair and Rula Lenska in *Snow White*.

Pantomime night is quite a long performance. The audience is there with the wish to be entertained and laugh at, or react to, what is on offer for the night. Live entertainment carries its own electricity and if an artist on stage has the audience with him then this is a worthwhile evening out. Bobby Davro was at Woking one year playing the part of "Who knows?" in the cast of "Can't Remember!" but he came on stage in one of the interludes in the pouch of a twelve-foot tall kangaroo and Dad has never laughed so much during a live theatre performance.

Another common aspect of the Woking pantomime is the interlude during a scene change where, to start with, some four characters are on stage in front of the curtains. It goes in a rather "He's behind you!" type of format.

Three characters act out a scene whilst totally ignoring the fourth, a ghoulishly clad ne'er-do-well character, as if they cannot see him at all. Of course, by now, the audience is well in with the joke.

The three sit on a bench giving it the "Yes he is – no he isn't" routine, ending with the refrain:

"Well then, we'll just have to do it again then – won't we... Whoops!"

Upon the "Whoops", the third character is carried off stage by the ghoul with the other two oblivious as to his fate.

Imagine then if you will, the frenzy the audience is in towards the end of the sketch, the children having been driven to distraction by the activities on stage, regular repetition of the phrase and the imminent denouement regarding the fate of the one remaining character when it is his time to face the ghoul.

By now, Chris is so excited, he is absolutely beside himself with unreserved, hysterical laughter. Surely the loudest in the audience and well done Chris for that. Laughter is the best medicine.

CHAPTER TWENTY-TWO

My Ship Sails In The Morning

People tend to resent and even ignore the passing of time, more so the older one gets.

They may consequently lay others open to being let down, inconvenienced, irritated or impacted by such lack of a responsible, considerate, attitude.

...And then there are autists.

Take Chris as an example. He feels the need to monitor and to mark time. It's a bit of a control thing really but it has become a matter of much amusement within the family. Everyone will be familiar with the salutation:

"Can you do this for me please? It's only a five-minute job."

Yes, agreed, rarely does the request meet the given timescale.

Well, to Chris, five minutes is five minutes, no more – no less. Famously in the past he has been commissioned on the basis of "Just a two minute job, please Chris." This resulting in frowns at the least, and a somewhat exasperated attitude in response to this patently unachievable activity. So Dad and Mum quickly dispensed with the initial two-minute job, graduated to five, and ultimately learnt to predicate requests for action by him on the basis that there was no reasonable timeline to be applied. They had come to know anyway that Chris remained on-task and would do the particular activity as soon as he could.

If he could not execute the activity for one reason or another, or due to some problem, he would not just sit there, perplexed. He would return to base, report his problem and request guidance as to the way forward. He would want to finish what he had been asked to do. Chris is an unavoidably conscientious soul.

When on family trips out in the car to a new location which might take some time to reach (think 'seaside' for example), at some mature stage of the journey there would come a plaintive cry from the back seats:

"Are we there yet?"

All parents have similar moments, no doubt, but in the case of Chris he would listen to the explanation and return to the pressing matter of achieving dominion over the current electronic game on his console or, more usually, return to his slumbers. He would not make a song-and-dance about it, since he had received his information and was almost always happy with just that. One other point of note is that he would rarely repeat the question during a subsequent journey to the same location, because he had already logged and processed the earlier information.

On occasions when the family was out and Chris was feeling as if he did not particularly want to be there, or if it was evidently going to be a long day, he would say:

"When are we going to leave to go home?"

This would usually be as soon as the party arrived at the destination. Given the response that it would be about 4 p.m., he would, upon the precise time of 4 p.m., announce this fact and expect that the party should be on the way home. Chris has never acknowledged the inexact science of the word 'about'.

He got his first watch when he was quite young. Wearing a watch was a great boon since he now had a direct correlation between a required schedule and his own need to be where he should be at the prescribed time. Travelling on the train became a more convenient, if not actually automatic, activity thanks to the ability to interface with the published timetable boards and electronically displayed platform timings.

Lunch at home for Chris was always at twelve o'clock midday whether Mum was ready or not. He circumvents this issue now by making his own sandwiches, thus avoiding the matter of possible conflict.

He has a constructive and resourceful attitude to time, time-keeping, watches, routine and time management in general. It really is how he manages each day's activities and a measure of how he copes with the precision required for those commitments outside direct parental control. (Think travel arrangements, lectures, meeting appointments and the like.) He is a great creature of habit.

"Chris...Just a minute!"

This request will now be met with a mock comical if not tolerant reaction designed to elicit a laugh, which it invariably does:

"It's been a minute!"

He has become quite a ham actor in the very best sense.

Evening meals have a reasonably well-established routine with some as a home take-away for him upstairs if there are no plans to have a sit-down meal together. Often, before meal times, he will present himself in the kitchen, go into one of those haughty, mock theatrical performances and announce (accompanied by suitable hand gestures)...

"My ship sails in the morning...I wonder what's for dinner?"

More laughter.

CHAPTER TWENTY-THREE

Give Him Every Chance

A pack of playing cards presents the opportunity for a game of chance. Then someone lays down a Joker. Well, it is clear enough to see where this thread is leading.

The family has their own Joker, dealt from the pack. Chris actually weighed-in on arrival at one and a half pounds heavier than his older brother. From the earlier deep concerns relating to his diagnosis, there is now only deep satisfaction that he is growing up to demonstrate truly life-affirming abilities and capabilities.

He has had obvious obstacles and difficulties fitting in with the established order of things. He is a really special person, healthy, highly intelligent and communicative. A credit to himself and those who have helped him to get to where he is today and wherever he might be going in the future.

A lot of effort has been expended by a lot of people to develop Chris's stimulation and interaction. Application of these criteria has been the prime mover in assisting his development. The family remains eternally grateful to all those who have been able to give their time to assist in this quest.

As parents they talked to teachers and classroom assistants over the years. Many of them have tried to explain the real pleasure they get when, after persisting with a course of study or instructions, the message finally drops with the pupil/student. These are the nuggets they cherish as autists do not generally regress and the learning stays in place. Undoubtedly these people have made a huge difference.

Those who were particularly close to him in the teaching sense clearly bonded with him at this mental level. The 'people magnet' that is Chris had evidently spun his web wisely.

Scope verses available restitution

How those with disabilities are accommodated in life, society, and the world in general is inseparably associated with diametrically opposed criteria. The identified need and the available cost of provision.

Satisfactory joint resolution of these two points is not always possible. In the majority of cases, compromise or a balanced approach is the plan.

The matter then passes on to a how-type-question which has an impact on everyone. Individuals, charities, councils, Parliament, the country and even the world, cannot yet present the case for the universal premise of utopian society. So what is to be done? There is an ever-widening need for money to accommodate a growing number of good causes and valid needs. Many people at every level of organised society do what they can but at the end of the day someone has to make a decision.

That decision is then invariably the cash one, based upon stretched provision and limited budget availability. This should be no surprise to anyone.

Yes, Chris is registered as disabled, though he is not as severely autistic as some. On behalf of those who know and love him, it would be inconceivable that he would have made anything of his life, certainly anything like the level of progress and development he has been able to learn, to reach and to achieve, without the vital guidance and assistance of those at Freemantles and Carwarden House in particular.

The matter of lack of money is a perennial problem. There is never enough available at the time, nor probably ever will be, to cater for everyone's needs now or in the future. If that provision of care and accommodation of autistic people is accepted as always coming down to a matter of cash-flow, if disabilities are to be catered for, then all should severally and equally supported. Regrettably this is not the case. The search for the ideal world continues. A world like that of *Star Trek – The Second Generation*, where at some stage in the future cost appears to be an irrelevant concept. We live in hope.

It is an inescapable thought that certain disabilities are more visual than others. Even today, autism is less visible than other disabilities though all disabilities are worthy of support are they not? Autists do not get the best deal, but all any concerned person is asking for is a fair deal. Surely that is not too much to ask for.

One of the earlier options offered to the family when Chris was at The Grove school, was whether he should actually be in mainstream education, rather than in one of the disability focused schools.

Parents by and large have the right to decide for themselves which school they would wish their children to attend. At that time, Chris's parents believed Freemantles to be the best option for him on the basis of their perception and review of the supporting information available. In some senses it was an easy decision to make. Yet because this was one which would have a fundamental impact on how and who he turned out to be, it was a hard decision and not entered into without considerable introspection. The needs of the child must surely be paramount here.

In Chris's case the parents remain convinced that disability-based schooling was the most appropriate provision for him.

Mainstream schooling may have been advantageous to local authority budgets but he simply would not be who he is today, nor have developed as much, nor achieved so much had he been consigned to full-time mainstream schooling at an early stage. At this stage of Chris's story, there is the firm conviction that the decision made a long time ago for him to go to Freemantles school in 1998 was the right one for him.

All decisions have consequences. The repercussions of him going there have been ultimately and universally positive for him. If he had gone in a different direction at that time, who knows what the result would have been? Nobody can say – but it is most unlikely to have been superior.

CHAPTER TWENTY-FOUR

University Year One – Foundation Year

The Computer Science (Games Programming) BSc (Hons) degree at Kingston University is a three-year course.

The qualifications Chris had achieved entitled him to be admitted directly to the first year of this course. In terms of his all-round development, however, it was felt appropriate to recommend that Chris took up the option of a Foundation Year, as a precursor. This would be an appropriate lead-in to the elevated academic world and lessen the impact of the initial learning curve. So three years would become four if all went well.

There was a great sense of anticipation all round.

Contacts had been previously established with the university and he was cleared to start his studies in the middle of September 2014.

Hoops to go through and a lot to organise

The family had previously been along to an Open Day at the Penrhyn Road campus in advance of the start of the university year.

All three of them had the opportunity to see the layout of the university and get an understanding of how the facilities were linked together. The temporary bulletin boards, the substantial number of helpers and the student ambassadors in place for the day were a great help in that regard. Chris made a point of viewing the content of the individual stalls of prospective student clubs and societies set up along the main concourse and within the rooms set aside for that purpose.

In one lecture theatre there was a presentation outlining the content of a typical course (Cyber Security in this case), along with how new students would be expected to interact with the lecturers to get the best out of their studies.

In the large and extensively provisioned computer-room laboratory, there was an explanation of the nature of direct software development and a chance for Chris to try out some of the kit, including re-visiting the new Occulus virtual reality headset. Current undergraduates were on hand here to show the nature, extent, and progress with games presently under development. Very interesting.

The more social aspects of university life and the manner in which students might approach them were laid out in a separate lecture theatre. Aspects discussed included accommodation, local amenities, travel, personal safety, security, emergency contact details, available student support, Students Union, general student funding, Freshers Week and the like.

The student support drop-in area on the ground floor was a stridently decorated pink-themed facility. A pre-arranged one-to-one consultation outlined the physical, mental, educational and pastoral support available to Chris, as well as that to which he was already entitled as a consequence of his condition. This was a comprehensive and pleasantly delivered presentation. Overall it was a long day trip but a most successful and worthwhile one.

Chris's first year at Kingston was actually to be spent at the

Kingston College building where there was a secure floor, floor ten, at the top of the building solely for university use being essentially a self-contained satellite facility. It was isolated from inadvertent access by mere college students by means of a swipe-card ID access security system. Naturally enough, however, certain common areas such as the refreshment canteen on the ground floor were open to all.

This Kingston College building, somewhat smaller than the main university campus, is a short distance further along Penrhyn Road and adjacent to Kingston Crown Court. Chris did not have the services of a scribe to attend classes with him to take lecture notes for his subsequent digestion and was to rely on his Royal Holloway College funded Dictaphone. This Dictaphone allowed him to be able to concentrate on presentation, format and content of the delivery in the lecture room and then to refer back to the audible record at his leisure.

During the summer prior to the start of Chris's studies, his buddy from Carwarden House days accompanied him on a number of preparatory dry-run expeditionary train and bus rides to and from Kingston University, to establish the development of independent travel.

Close family friend Bob, having his own chauffeur business near the family home, was commissioned to assist with travel arrangements. Funded taxi support for certain of Chris's journeys was available and found to be especially helpful on days where Chris would be finishing lectures late in the day.

These taxi fares were partly funded by the disability side of Student Finance where, although the family had to make payment initially, reimbursement of the running costs occurred regularly enough to make this arrangement most acceptable and very convenient. This was a great boon and enabled Chris to make his start to university life in as safe and secure a way as could have reasonably been expected. There was total trust in who was driving him home at whatever time. Mum continued with her commission of taking him to the train station most mornings.

Taxi funding was to cease after this first year. The lack of such funding for the future would have some impact on any decision relating to transport needs. However, there was only one thought at the time.

"Let's get through the first year first."

Before the start of the university year there were two further points of note. Firstly, in August, there was a week's university familiarisation course at the separate Kingston Hill, Coombe Road faculty of the university. This was still in Kingston but quite some way from the Penrhyn Road campus. The short course was open by invitation to those disabled students who it was believed would benefit from additional support in order to meet their full potential during their time at the university.

The course went by the rather grand title of 'Compact Scheme and Care Leaver Support & Head Start Summer School' under the responsibility of the overall 'Compact Scheme' by the university. The scope of the course and available pastoral care for Chris and others covered, but was not necessarily limited to, the following:

1. A single point of contact for information, advice and guidance through the application, transition and enrolment process and throughout the duration of studies at the university.
2. Preparation for student life and support for transition to Kingston University.
3. Regular opportunities to keep in touch with the Compact Scheme team through such as campus drop-in sessions (pit-stops), newsletters, emails and phone calls.
4. Workshops and conferences designed to motivate and equip students with the skills needed to succeed

at the University and beyond (covering study skills, money matters and employability).

5. Notification of extra-curricular activities such as Student Ambassador and Student Associate schemes.

6. Support in the event of approaching graduation.

Chris was eligible for the course and was in receipt of an invitation to attend.

He was keen to go. It was not so convenient for his parents to go to this additional week with Chris, so the thought was that, as a real adventure, he might like to go on his own provided suitable, safe, and secure transport could be arranged. Bob and Trevor's taxis were organised for him but he would indeed be on his own there with no buddy for the duration.

Here was a chance to gain additional insight into university life and benefit from the experience of greater independence and familiarisation with the travel route to and from Kingston.

Chris's response at the end of the week was that he was glad he had gone on the course. He found it useful and said it had been fun and helpful.

The second point of note related to an optional feature available to all students preceding the start of studies. This custom may be much revered by students although, for mostly prosaic reasons, they might have trouble recalling the actual day-to-day content, as they might quite possibly have been partially or completely under the influence of an uninhibited consumption of alcohol. By this is meant, Freshers Week.

Chris had no interest in the alcoholic aspect of this exercise by virtue of his disposition, nor would he have had an overly concerned inclination to investigate the social aspects of liaising with other students that the week might be expected to afford. He decided to forego Freshers Week.

Mid-September 2014 came soon enough.

***

Welcome to Kingston University. "Chris, you're good to go!"

After the understandable settling-in period at the university, Chris appeared to accept the now considerable extension to his working day and bonded well enough with his new routine. The train and bus transport worked well both ways, with the additional planned periodic support of Bob's taxis to rely on with no significant problems.

In trying to think of things from Chris's point of view, here was an altogether bigger place. A greater extent of things to cope with, but above all, a place to absorb knowledge and gain a measure of increased awareness in respect of the wider world in general.

As a means of keeping his parents in touch with his itinerary, Chris would provide an outline of his working day, particularly when individual aspects might be giving him cause for concern. One way of easing his mind at such times was to talk to him and break down the problem, be it social or academic. To break it down into smaller and hopefully more manageable chunks. If he could rationalise and resolve these smaller portions, then he would be closer to an overall solution by the simple expedient of reconnecting all the small pieces into a reconciled whole. The term 'simple' has been used here, yet the concept of integral calculus is implied for this exercise.

> *(Dad here:*
> *Chris would run a mile if you threw him a curved ball by asking him what an integral was, especially when he would understand this as a maths related question. But if you described the mechanism in terms of producing a jigsaw picture from its pile of individual constituent pieces, then*

he would get the message. Whether he would be minded to actually address such an activity might be another matter entirely.)

Interaction with university academic life, and the sequencing and scheduling of the scope of individual pieces of work at this level, was as new to his parents as it was to him. The demarcation here though was that knowledge of the actual status of the work he was involved with was now unavoidably and clearly just for him to report. He was now solely responsible for this aspect of his studies.

The matter of schedule reared its head more than once with Chris's deliverables. He would only tend to point out that he might be having a schedule problem at the time he had the problem, not that he might have a schedule problem at a certain time in the future. This would usually require some nifty consequential parental support in order to avoid irreparable disasters, sometimes as a close shave and invoking subsequent parental retreat to a glass of red wine.

"Chris, we are working on a need-to-know basis here – but first we need to know if we need to know."

Focus...focus

The first year Foundation Year comprised four modules. Whilst for subsequent years there was a measure of choice regarding selection of differing modules based on aptitude, ability and choice, all students on the Foundation Year undertook the same modules.

Foundation Year module subjects:

1) Technical Investigation and Skills
2) Computer Programming
3) Computer Systems
4) Maths for Computing

Module 4 included the requirement for Chris to take and pass 'A' level maths. Here now was a real challenge. Maths coursework had been submitted during the year though there was still the matter of the exam. This took place towards the end of the academic year and proved a fail in terms of achieving the necessary minimum classification of a grade 'C', in order to qualify to progress to the next year of the course.

His result was close enough to the required grade for the exam that the university offered him a resit. Time was pressing, nevertheless the deed was done. The result though would not be known until the time of the Freshers Week for the following academic year.

An unavoidably uncomfortable time was had by all in the interim. Not so much so for Chris though since, in paraphrasing the mantra given many times by his parents:

"All I can do is my best and that is what I have done."

He would not be on any guilt trip nor should he. Dad and Mum wanted no more than that he should have done his best. Chris, as ever, took it all in his stride.

To his own great credit and the somewhat stunned reaction of his parents when the results finally came through, this challenge was met. Wow!

A mighty close run thing, no doubt, but...now back to the red wine.

A start to submissions

As part of his Maths for Computing module course work, he had to prepare and submit a statistical analysis, by way of a pukka report, relating to a comparison of the ambient temperature conditions of a whole range of cities. The range of cities was worldwide and across various regions and countries. The premise was to outline temperature ranges for a range of cities against their elevation above sea level and location in terms of latitude plus any consequential relationships between them, as bidden by the required scope of work.

Actually he had so far never yet actually written a report like that in his life. A slight problem.

Chris had a reasonable though not unlimited time in which to submit this piece of work. The first knowledge about this at home was when he offered what he had done as a draft for parental review. The view was that the family were a little concerned.

"Could do better. Let the dog see the rabbit," said Dad. Chris provided details of the original scope of work. He had evidently taken on board what had been explained in the lecture but had misinterpreted certain questions relating to the content of parts of the work. He had also not taken proper account of the given table of marks available for each valid individual aspect of the report.

So here was the matter in hand – to help but not to do the work for him.

This resolved into breaking down the work into bite-sized chunks, and even small nibbles where necessary, to see how far he was able to go in satisfying the table of marks set in each case for each part of the work.

He provided a front cover sheet and title block for 'x' marks; a contents sheet for 'x' marks; pagination for 'x' marks; individual graphs with tagged ordinates and abscissa for 'x' marks; consistent font styling for 'x' marks; formulation of responses to individual questions…and so on.

He addressed each aspect assiduously, with as much repetition as was appropriate and was happy with what he had produced at the end of the exercise. There were one or two points that he could probably have improved further but because he was happy with what he had done, and time was short, then that was what was submitted to be marked.

As Chris has not offered reports for parental review on other subjects to any significant degree since that time, he definitely learnt something from the delivery of this activity. He was subsequently to advise that his submission of this piece of work was deemed quite satisfactory by the powers that be. This then represented a great improvement on what had been his earlier draft submission. That earlier work would, by default, have had to be the one to be marked by the faculty, possibly resulting in an unsatisfactory mark. Chris had had the presence of mind to raise the issue in the first place, so credit to him for his level of improved performance here.

He would have to pass all four modules to be able to progress to the next year's studies, all being well.

His results for this Foundation Year 2014/2015 saw him achieve a 57% average mark over the four modules at 'Level 3'. The corresponding reaction from home was much relief and significant legitimate pride for Chris in having taken this first step (nay: leap) on this new, exciting, challenging and, hopefully, ultimately successful enterprise.

One weekend, as was their wont, Dad, Mum and Chris were out for a Saturday morning coffee. Chris was being gently interrogated as to how he was getting on with this totally new adventure and the challenges he might be facing. Chris was in no less than confident, if not actually, effusive form. This was good news because, although he might have difficulty in reading the body language of others, when it came to parental observation then, by virtue of many years careful study, they had come to know how to read him well enough. He was relaxed and at ease.

He felt that he was settling in well, thanks in no small part to the earlier pre-planning and research done about university life, the curriculum and travel arrangements. Essentially he felt fully pre-prepared for university life and was already comfortable with it, with the likelihood of "What do I do now?" circumstances much reduced.

He went on to explain what he had learnt about computer binary coding at his first week's lectures for one of his modules. This, he expanded, related to the movement of a subject to the right by saying:

"Go left, go left, go left."

At this point parental eyes rolled and…

"Time for another coffee I think."

CHAPTER TWENTY-FIVE

University Year Two

This was the first proper year of his course, following on from the Foundation Year. Chris was to take the Computer Science (Games Programming) degree course with the following module descriptions within the structure of the syllabus.

1) Business Analysis & Solution Design
2) Games Science
3) Object Oriented Programming
4) Computer Games Systems

With the lapsing of the funding for him he was now to be even more self-reliant in terms of transport. Logistics comprised a morning parental lift to the local train station for him to catch the train to Surbiton where he had to cross a very busy main road, make sure he selected the correct number bus for the university campus and board the bus using his Oyster card.

His mission was to get to university safely and in a consistently punctual manner within the time schedule dictated by his timetable. It was also necessary he should return to the home train station in like manner at the end of the day to be picked up by Mum (mainly). This journey became easier and easier with increased familiarity. The mobile phone proved a great benefit. 'Taxi Bob' would only need to be an emergency consideration from now on.

Chris was more and more resourceful, but in order for him to fully appreciate the range of actions available to him in the event of a transport problem, he had to be exposed to as many of those possible options as could be envisaged in advance. The thought occurred that if more than one problem arose within the same time frame, he would just have to cope.

Mum contends that multi-tasking is primarily a characteristic more associated with the female psyche than the male of the species. This may be open to review and discussion but Dad merely demurs at this stage. In any event, Chris had to be exposed to a degree of pre-programming in order for him to be able to recognise that there was a problem in the first place.

Happily he had successfully progressed in his studies from the Foundation Year and now needed a range of dry-runs over the summer break to reinforce the imprint of the experience of travelling by train to and from Kingston and the short bus ride to the university campus. This was important because the taxi support would no longer be funded for him and he would now have to be largely self-reliant. Chris coped well with these trips and the lessons learned, the alternative train options and the range of bus numbers which applied to him. His Carwarden House buddy was again prevailed upon to accompany him on these trips by way of mentoring.

Chris appeared reasonably content with the details, although the first few trips in earnest would obviously be of concern to his parents. The journeys to and from home to the nearest train station remained a parental responsibility, which also cut down the overall time of the journey. He needed to be able to keep train tickets and Oyster cards separate and safe on his person.

He had a new campus to get used to as he was now at the

main university site, with this being a slightly shorter bus journey from Surbiton Station than that for the Kingston College building. He was closer to student support facilities but had new coursework, new fellow students, new lecturers and a new timetable to accommodate.

It was some time later that the parents became aware of a situation that was quite amusing in the schadenfreude sense and one which in all probability could not have been predicted by mere neuro-typicals like Dad or Mum. Admittedly Chris would have had a lot on his mind but what would an autist do? Well, he would need to concentrate on what he knew and had established in his brain and changes to those practices would require new input.

Chris said that with the location of his studies now being on the main campus, he would leave after the last lecture to get the bus back to Kingston College further up the road, where he would get off and then get a separate bus from there back to Surbition station. By this mechanism he would directly pass by the main campus on the way to the station.

"Ha! Not what you need to do, Chris."

Happily Dad and Mum always laughed with him and not at him.

When they had finally picked themselves up off the floor, they were able to explain that he should get the bus direct to Surbiton station from just outside the campus. This is akin to turning left when one gets on a long-haul flight to get the premium-economy section rather than turning right to access the economy section, (though people who have not flown that far in the past will not have a clue what is meant by this).

This change in bus activity would save up to thirty minutes on his journey time to home. It is as a general rule very important to know where you are going and where you have come from. This is rather reminiscent of the famous 'The Bricklayer's Lament' by Gerard Hoffnung as presented to the Oxford Union in 1958

– quite one of the funniest things ever heard on radio. Check it out on You Tube.

Chris would still be using his Dictaphone, but now had the additional and valued support of a lecture note-taker assigned to him by the university. This would be a student sitting with him in his lectures, so that he could concentrate on the lecture itself and yet have the benefit of those third-party notes to refer to afterwards. The note-taker would receive a stipend for this activity paid separately by the university. Chris had to liaise with whosoever was to be his note-taker for each lecture, each day, and arrange a meeting time and place prior to each lecture. He got a lot out of this system and found his note-takers amenable, most capable and greatly efficient in posting the notes on to him by email afterwards.

Plans to be made

End of year results for this second year were satisfactory. Chris achieved an average of 52% over the four modules at 'Level 4'.

The itinerary for the following year (year three of four), brought to mind that the original synopsis of the modules for the course rather underplayed the extent of detailed programming, coding and pure maths in terms of the work to be covered.

Dad and Mum were quite prepared to hold their hands up here to the extent that they were effectively the prime movers responsible for analysing this part of the course for, and with, Chris. With the benefit of hindsight they did not do it as comprehensively as they might have done right at the early stages of his initial entry into university life.

Chris thought about this for some time, consulted, researched and concluded that he wished to progress next year on the basis of a modest change of direction. He wanted to move to the Information Systems (Internet Business) course.

Everyone at Kingston gave sterling support and guidance during this period of re-assessment and the university itself was obviously accepting of the final decision. No doubt they would have not allowed the change to go ahead if they had reservations about his ability to undertake the work. Chris ended up being well suited to the revised situation. In essence he had achieved his intended extraction from the engine room of lots and lots of maths.

His somewhat matter-of-fact but nonetheless appropriate observation at the successful conclusion to these rearrangements was:

"I'm more of a Van Gogh than an Einstein."

CHAPTER TWENTY-SIX

University Year Three

...A slight change of course

Having successfully redirected his course for this year to Information Systems (Internet Business) and on entering the second year of the three-year course, Chris's modules were to be as follows:

1) Networking & Operating Systems
2) Database & UML Modelling
3) Electronic & Web-Based Business Processes
4) Projects & Their Management

Knowing that Chris does not get nervous it has to be said, however, that he will admit to feeling apprehensive at times. This is due to that aspect of his condition which still limits his ability to pre-recognise or imagine experiences he has not yet had. The older he gets, the more understanding he has and the better are his chances of reducing or managing such apprehension(s). This might infer he does not suffer misapprehension. This is possible. He still has a need to understand...but in his own way.

Chris was confident that his course work marks were generally up to scratch. He was understandably rightly pleased with this aspect of the year's progress, being confident but not over-confident. He logged the end-of-term exam dates and the family talked about the best way of revising for each of the exams. The suggestion was that he should take on the discipline of concentrating on each subject in turn and bit by bit rather than flogging away at one subject in isolation.

It had constantly been pointed out to him in terms of exams that, when in the exam room, he needed to understand what he was being asked to do and that he should always only try to do his best.

One important aspect here was the need to emphasise to Chris that he would need to revise all elements of his study work once he had been able to reduce them to bite-sized pieces. This was a philosophy previously instilled in him, but one worth repeating as many times as possible. He would also have to revisit his revision 'bits' more than once, several times in fact, to ensure that as much as possible remained in his head and would therefore be easier to recall during the exam.

The revisiting revision concern was uppermost in Dad and Mum's minds at the time. They were only too aware of Chris's historical one-time-only approach to matters of brain consultation and information retention. It was felt that this emphasis on repetition, and yet more repetition, would aid self-confidence and a feeling of being more comfortable with each of the particular subjects during the exams.

Exam preparation on the day was covered with him in detail. He needed to be properly prepared, be as comfortable as possible with each subject and be relaxed before walking into the exam room.

Chris was well up to speed for the forthcoming first exam, Networking & Operating Systems, as he had given this work special consideration. Half the exam paper was given over to written text responses, to which he had applied significant revision and it was the one exam which he regarded as the biggest challenge for that very reason. Did this prove to be problematic? Well – not in practice.

He returned to the family home evidently pleased with what he had done in the exam. He reported that three questions needed to be answered out of the four posted on the exam paper, but just before the end of the exam he realised that he had actually answered all four.

"Muppet!"

He went on to say that he walked out of the room telling the invigilator what he had done and advising which of his responses should be ignored when marking his paper. It will never be known what, if any, notice was taken of this entreaty but it is not at all difficult to imagine a winsome, if not slightly bemused, expression on the face of said invigilator at the time. After all, Chris really does have an impact wherever he goes.

The second exam, Database & UML Modelling, was a subject dear to his heart. There was, however, to be a separate challenge here because the exam was to be held at a location off-campus in a church. Not a particular problem for mere non-autists, but Chris was going to have to find out where this was and, more importantly, have some confidence that he would be able to find it on the day and at the correct time for the exam. It was easy enough to find on the map at home and he could see it well enough whilst the route was jointly reviewed several times to show how he was going to get there. No problem at the time. The actual problem though was putting him in the physical situation of being able to walk to it.

So having solved the 'find' question, there was for him the more prosaic matter of putting one foot in front of the other to actually get there. He solved this conundrum himself by the intelligent step of approaching someone at the student help-desk who was only too happy to walk him round there in advance one lunchtime. This was a great help because Chris would normally only need to be shown the way once. Although he is no elephant, he does not forget.

The third event was the Electronic & Web-Based Business Processes exam, set for Monday 8th May 2017, Chris's last exam in this academic year. Again, the location was to be off-campus but this time at the local TA Army Centre. There were similar parental concerns as to the logistics involved here. However, Chris had gone to the Disability Centre at the university, this time to be given a map, and he proceeded to walk round in his lunch hour to find where the exam was to be held, in advance of the exam date and, not only that, but to find his way back to the campus. Clever bunny.

Chris took great pleasure in reporting that there would not actually be an exam for the fourth module, Projects & Their Management. This was a subject solely based on coursework progress and achievement throughout the academic year. The subject was a group-based workshop production with an initial prototype status presentation early in the year. An alpha presentation followed later in the year to show the stages of development and a beta presentation was made on Tuesday 9th May 2017, giving the final results of the work group. Chris provided his own verbal report to the invigilators for this event in company with the other members of the group.

Sadly, not all the other members of the group appeared to treat the subject with the same commitment as Chris. He was rather let down by two group members habitually not participating in the progress of the group's ongoing workshop work, and who did not then even actually participate in this final presentation. However, he and the truncated numbers of the presentation party had done enough of the historical group work to fulfil the scope of the final presentation and successfully achieve the level of a 'pass' for the module. Thank goodness.

The year's semester officially ended on 24th June. Soon afterwards Chris got his full results for the year from the University. He had averaged 50% over the four modules at 'Level 5' with no retakes. He was so rightly pleased with what he had done and what he had achieved. He got big hugs from Dad and Mum. Good man.

Languages and accounts

After the hiatus of the exam period, thoughts returned to an earlier matter Chris had brought up in March prior to the exams. He was concerned about PHP coding. This is a computer programming language drawing on several sources to build a website. It is essentially designed to evaluate forms of data sent from a browser, build custom web content to serve the browser, talk to a database and send and receive cookies. It does not, however, make the tea as well. When he has the picture of the website in his mind, then all is clear to him and he can directly change the format, presentation and impact of the website, along with outline links and paths on the site.

Programming languages are de-facto prime elements of this level of study. However, Chris was inclined towards changing aspects of his studies for the next year in order to keep exposure to such aspects to a minimum – there were to be choices available. He had done well enough this year though.

One other element of the academic work process this year proved that Chris still had a way to go to be in complete control of his needs. Within the Projects & Their Management module, he had forgotten that there was to be an in-class test one day as a part of the course work. This meant that, not only was he under-revised for this event, but the actual test took him somewhat by surprise. By a measure of good fortune, whilst his module overall mark might have otherwise been rather higher if he had been properly prepared, he still achieved the level of a 'pass' for it.

Chris had also not been aware that there was to be a meeting held after one of the year's exams in April regarding study options for the following year. He only found out later that he had missed this meeting, but was not to worry because, whilst a face-to-face meeting is always best for communication and comprehension, the tutor sent out the reference material by email. There was a whole shed-load of pages which nearly crippled the home printer.

Well, to be fair about the lack of notice, there was probably a general statement made to the students about the meeting by some means or other. The concern again here is that, because it may not have been mentally acknowledged by Chris to have been directed to him as well for whatever reason, then the import of the message may not have registered with him either. This relates back to his earlier school and college experiences. No great damage done, but he should somehow have been able to make himself aware of the situation in the first place. This was not the first such example of mislaid awareness and it would probably not be the last.

As with his earlier years at Kingston, Chris maintained a 100% attendance record for the year's study. With everything he had to cope with here and elsewhere, this is commendable, and a measure of his application and intent. Against this there is the unavoidable observation that the cost of this year's course, £9,000, represents a charge related to a period at University of effectively no more than seven months out of the twelve. This charge would rise to £9,250 for the next year.

On Thursday 5th May 2017 there was a home visit by Rachel Pearson of the NAS (National Autistic Society). Chris's NAS support was funded by SFE (Student Finance England) as a part of their Disability Unit. The purpose of the visit was to sort out with Chris his final year Dissertation Project for 2018. Dad kept out of the way by the simple expedient of being at work, but the visit was deemed very helpful and coloured by Rachel's opinion that Chris was hard-working, committed, and fun to liaise with. Mum thought Rachel was a lovely lady who had him summed up just right (but in a nice way).

Rachel was interested in helping Chris assess the various options available for this final year project. She was rightly of the view that Chris needed further clarification on the depth of the subject options so he would be in a position to reach an appropriate conclusion. The extent of guide information from the rather limited precis scripts offered against the suggested subjects in the available web-based downloads was considered inadequate. She would talk to various lecturers across the IT faculty at Kingston and report back to Chris. The information trail rather petered out at this stage.

This dissertation project would need an authority or a mentor at the university by way of support. Such a provision would be available to all students, so Chris here would be neither especially advantageously supported, nor actually disadvantaged. He would be on the same nominal level of support as his co-students.

As a follow-up to this year's activities, Chris along with a parent (i.e. Mum) was invited by the Disability Unit to attend the university for an Open Day in August. They were to act as support mentors on a consultative panel brought together to talk about steps needed to be taken by prospective university students with disabilities. These steps related to the transition to university with associated DLA (Disability Living Allowance) funding and the like.

★★★

Additional features

Two small, though quite telling aspects, of Chris's ever-growing development came to light in the year. Outside the ever-present parental concentration on observations within the realms of autism, they may well have passed without particular thought in the conventional world.

Aspect 1: The local Sainsbury's store has a very acceptable canteen upstairs. Shopping trips are predicated by refreshments of one sort or the other at this upstairs emporium. Chris would usually choose a drink from the range on display which normally covered one or more of his favourite options.

In this instance, his options were zilch, zippo, null and void. The available choices came under the heading of esoteric to say the least. Chris paused.

"I'll have Cranbury and Lime. I think I'm going to be adventurous today," he said.

"Huhh – good luck with that then," was Dad's observation.

So what does Dad know anyway? Chris has always been encouraged to at least try things, and has been constantly assured that there would never be a problem if he did not like what he had chosen, but had at least tried. He polished off the bottle and announced himself well satisfied with his choice. Another step forward.

Aspect 2: Around spring-time there was a TV programme called *Bigheads*. Here members of the public competed in fancy dress under a range of scenarios, mostly rather wet and ridiculously reminiscent of pantomime, for the privilege of having the opportunity of winning a not inconsiderable sum of money. The real point here was that contestants had to wear large, hollow, polystyrene caricature heads, of entertainment artists, politicians or sports people.

That it was mayhem and a fun family event was true. That is was patently ridiculous was unavoidable. Any such mayhem, part hosted by the ebullient Kriss Akabusi, is always going to be good entertainment. The thing here was that Chris would be laughing heartily at the cod antics on the screen. Evidence, if any was needed, that he has fully developed his appreciation of the absurd and the utterly ridiculous.

CHAPTER TWENTY-SEVEN

University Year Four

...How near – how far?

So here it was – finally – the last one – the important one – the really **big** one. Chris had come so far, so far, but this if all went well would be the measure of the man.

For heaven's sake, this lovely autistic charmer of a man was to take the last year of a BSc Honours degree course. So many hopes and good wishes went with him from so many people who knew of him, his current condition, and this stage of his life, that the thought might have been he could not possibly fall short. But, as is well known, if wishes, hopes, and dreams, were stable currency nobody would fail any challenge. This is not how it works, however, in the real world.

The proof of the man might be helped by support, but would be proved or not proved by him, and him alone, on the basis of the studies undertaken, reports submitted and exams taken this year. The hope, of course, was that he would achieve a creditable, full working measurement of his abilities to his own satisfaction, in what in all probability, would be his last year of university study.

Dad and Mum have been party to their own work-in-progress, their own living experiment so to speak. It will continue to be an ongoing experiment in that, whilst observations may be drawn, no conclusions can be finalised because the game is not yet at an end, irrespective of what may or may not be achieved this academic year.

By now they have a greater depth of knowledge and understanding of autism, an aspect of life that affects so many people in so many different ways and to differing degrees. Both are gratified that autism, the 'invisible disability', appears to be more and more recognised for what it represents to the wider world today.

Dad and Mum have been privy to a growing level of awareness within Chris in so many ways that might have been but a pipe dream only a few short years ago. Well done, son.

In the words of Buzz Lightyear from *Toy Story*:

"To infinity and beyond!"

Or to quote another phrase from an altogether different era, courtesy of J M Barrie, the way to Neverland is:

"Second star to the right and straight on 'til morning."

Chris himself would put no arbitrary limit in place here. He some time ago came across the theory and concept of parallel universes and constantly brings this up when involved in relevant conversations.

A Dream Catcher was purchased in America some time ago. These are generally of a hooped shape, being an established tradition of a number of native-American tribes and are intended to protect the sleeping individual from negative dreams whilst letting positive dreams through. The positive dreams would slip through the hole in the centre of the hanging device and glide down the feathers to the person sleeping below. The negative dreams would get caught up in the web, and expire when the first rays of the sun struck them. So much for a Dream Catcher; Dad and Mum would like to think that one day someone would invent a Dream Launcher.

The layout, development and recording of this whole narrative of Chris's tale has nearly caught up with real time. As of now, Chris is in his final year (probably) at Kingston University, whilst the writing of this stage of the book is almost in competition with current events. It remains to be seen if he will get to the end of this academic year before the book is finished.

Project prospective profile

At the end of the previous year's study, the university provided a comprehensive range of 'special project' suggestions from which Chris could choose a main project for his final year. The need here was for students to be able to draw together the lessons and principles learned during the preceding years and demonstrate them in a suitable, original, way as a meaningful and useful piece of work of demonstrable merit.

Most of the project options involved a degree of computer coding, some a higher level of coding than others but very few with no coding at all. Some were internet-web-based with others more spreadsheet-based, with or without networking and information management. All were effectively on the basis of the student being able to build something.

Chris was minded to choose an option that did not require much coding and this still left a useful range of some seven options open to him from the original basis of selection. At home these options were discussed and viewed from all angles by and with Chris.

Then came yet another 'light bulb' moment...

Good opportunities so rarely present themselves at the most appropriate time and here was the thing. The drop-dead date for selection of his final-year project was approaching the status of uncomfortable proximity at the time the family went to the live Extreme Robot show in Guildford in June 2017.

This saw the concept of *Robot Wars* elevated by an order of magnitude (and then some) to an entirely different scale of content, presentation, treatment and professionalism over that encountered all that time ago in Legoland. Well, not to put too fine a point on it, Chris was enthused by the entire set-up.

The thought was, he might be able to do a project based around these robot machines, their interaction, set-up, performance and the rest...but how would that go down with the university?

That very evening Chris wrote to the tutor assigned as his university mentor and received a response confirming the prospective format of his planned project would indeed fulfil the brief. Suddenly he had the working basis of an acceptable format for his final year project and, unequivocally, he had a driving personal enthusiasm for the subject. Motivation would not be a problem.

As a separate exercise, Chris had made contact with those responsible for the franchise itself and received a receptive, supportive and constructive response. In essence, they were quite happy to give consent for him to produce his planned work utilising the name and premise of the franchise as the basis for his project. They liked his idea enough to say that, upon completion of the work, there was every possibility that they would look into integrating his software within the company web site for all to access. What a result that would be. Let's hope it comes to fruition.

Before reviewing the enthralling Extreme Robot show, it is appropriate that his modules for the final year should be reported.

The planned study work for his final year would be as follows:

1) Digital Business
2) Internet Security
3) Advanced Databases and the Web
4) Individual Project (The Final Year Project)

Chris started his final year of university study enthusiastically, keen to get the initial details of schedule, course content and timetables established in his routine. He was due to attend University every day, Monday to Friday, at differing times each day. Not only that, but his Friday workshop, the only attendance that day, was from four to six in the afternoon meaning more time was spent travelling than actually being at University. A bit of a mixed routine and shorter lecture durations, but this would make it easier to spend some extra time at the LRC (Learning Resource Centre) if need arose. He was again to have the assistance of note takers during lectures and at least some of his peer group from last year's studies were still around.

There was light at the end of the tunnel in terms of the five day university commitment. A timetable change in January 2018 moved his one lecture on a Thursday to a Monday. Thursday attendance was thus no longer obligatory. Monday now was to be a very full day of attendance, from 9 a.m. to 6 p.m., but he was back to four days a week.

By the fourth year of university life, undergraduates would be left more and more to their own devices, rightly taking more responsibility for their own actions. Chris had continued support from Rachel, his NAS supporter, by virtue of a weekly one-hour meeting at the university, from individual lecturers as and when required, and from his parents of course. He was constantly reminded that if he had a problem, concern or lack of understanding of any particular task at university, then he had to formulate and compile the concern into the right form of words, so that he could organise the way in which to request resolution from the appropriate source.

What is being said here is that Chris, in spite of his development and the evidence that he has a very open and enquiring mind, knows what he knows but can become concerned about what he does not know. In a nutshell, this is the ultimate chicken and egg situation. (Ed: "Enough with the yokes already!") The mechanism here is to help Chris to know what he needs to know. This is getting easier; it really is.

Module 4, the final year Individual Project, has significant importance in terms of the measurement of a student's ability and the effort required to achieve the goal of a successful degree. In Chris's case, of course, this would be based upon his Extreme Robot experience.

The official marks for submission of the initial scope of the work were advised early in November 2017 (if memory serves). These comprised 10% of his total marks for the project. He achieved 61% which, of course, meant he now had 6.1% of the marks towards his final result. How he actually performed at the end of the final year remains to be seen.

A big interest...

Since this *Robot Wars*-based activity was to form such an important part of the final year of his degree course, it is as well to provide some background here regarding the extent of his interest.

Chris was excited by the return of *Robot Wars* to the TV screen with two brand new and even more combative series in July 2016 and then 2017. It had initially been broadcast on BBC Two from February 1998 to February 2001 and then on Channel 5 from

November 2003 to 28 March 2004. Chris had become a great devotee. It was a double bonus that another great favourite, Dara O'Briain, was the face of the new programmes.

This *Robot Wars* feature is no 'Mickey Mouse' operation. It is about as far removed from a gentle game of conkers as can be imagined.

The Extreme Robot live show in June 2017 was a two-hour mix of 'bot (robot) mayhem and very much along the lines of the television show – loud music – presenters active and loud – vocal audience interaction – very professionally run – high quality transparent arena wall giving complete safety of the audience – floor flipper – floor pit – flame grating grill – floor spikes – speeding 'bots thudding into each other.

Some of the 'bots from the television show were there at Guildford. With all the other 'bots, they could be viewed close up, thankfully in passive mode, during the intermission tour through the garage pit area behind the arena. Under arena battle conditions, of course, they would give out plenty of crash, bang and wallop – another sensory overload.

Those who have made the acquaintance of the *Robot Wars* shows on TV will be familiar enough with these confrontational and impressively engineered robots. Those who have not may only contemplate the build-up to the opening contest.

Sunday 22nd October 2017 saw the return of *Robot Wars* to BBC television for a new series and Chris had this date logged in some time ago. His excitement, wedged between Dad and Mum on the sofa, was only eclipsed by his increased volume.

Think *VERY LOUD* and imagine the enthusiastic, ebullient, Jonathon Pearce starting off the conflict commentary with the following strident call to arms.

"Roboteers – are you ready?"

"Three!"

"Two!"
"One!"
"ACTIVATE!"

The assigned driver(s) for each team engaged their remote-control consoles to release their combatants into battle from the safe vantage point of an overhead control room. This location provided a full view of the arena floor, the floor obstacles and more. The complete arena perimeter protection comprised two panels of transparent polycarbonate safety shielding.

Speedy – yes.

Noisy – yes.

Frantic – yes.

Robust – yes.

Powerful – yes.

Gladiatorial – yes.

Intriguing – yes.

Spectacular – yes.

Entertaining – certainly.

Each bout comprised three minutes of unrestrained conflict, absolute mayhem, carnage, spinning, weaving, smashing, crashing, flipping and hammering at speed between these weighty machines, all bent upon superiority or survival by any means possible. Two ginormous house robots, typically Matilda and Dead Metal (with duties occasionally shared by other house robots such as Sir Killalot and Shunt) guarded opposite corners of the arena floor during these battles. They would render their own version of summary justice on any robot reckless enough to venture within range during the proceedings.

These remote controlled, motorised, robots are complex pieces of machinery. They are built mainly of metal, to high standards of construction, employing close engineering tolerances. There are generic construction categories such as Flipper, Spinner, Crusher and Axe Bot and they are built with much care and great attention to detail by teams of people who take the whole shebang to a high level of commitment and quality of hardware. Combatants shake hands after each bout happy to have done their best. Teams and team members carry on a large degree of genuine mutual team support away from the arena floor after battling.

Such respect is heartening in today's world. This provides an opportunity for a large degree of learning, engineering research, development and cross-fertilisation of ideas. Propulsion and weaponry are generally gas powered by CO^2 (carbon dioxide). Both propulsion and weaponry are vulnerable to damage by attack, resulting in possible failure by virtue of immobility or even destruction in the arena. Mortality is therefore an ever present possibility for the 'bots.

The extent of defence mechanisms and shielding built into the design of these robots has no little bearing on their ability to survive individual contests. Those petrol-heads with an interest in motor cars in the outside world will be familiar with the term 'power to weight ratio'. This, simplistically, relates the available speed and efficiency of a vehicle to the weight it has been designed to carry. Robot development has to balance the provision of defence attributes against the nature of installed offensive capabilities. As in life, this is a matter of judgement and balance.

In terms of the house robots, Sir Killalot is the strongest and most feared. In his present guise he weighs in at 741 kilogrammes. He has a top speed of 10 mph and formidable high strength steel armour as the prime means of defence. For attack armaments, he has an attack rotating drill, the capability to lift 300 kilogrammes in each of his arms, whilst his claws are able to apply 2.5 tonnes of crushing force. This somewhat imposing beast of a machine is rarely challenged during bouts in the arena, other than by default. The best defence against Sir Killalot is for combatant robots to run away – if they can. He has been an ever present feature in the franchise since series two.

By comparison, house robot Matilda is less of a brute than Sir Killalot and has also been a permanent fixture in each series to date. One of the ways combatants can accrue points is by the nature and amount of aggression they are able to demonstrate. Attacking house robots, albeit at risk to themselves, is therefore an option during bouts. Competitor robots have been known to attack Matilda but generally without achieving notable damage or inflicting ignominy. Only Flipper style 'bots have been able to achieve the planned objective of putting her on her back (and rarely so at that).

Back to the matter of Guildford. The family was fortunate enough to secure three tickets from the limited availability of VIP tickets for the live show in 2018. Their second visit. During the interval they would be able to visit the robot pit area behind the arena where all the team preparation and repair work takes place and this time it would be possible for Chris to actually drive one of these awesome beasts. He could not wait...he simply could not wait.

A look at Chris, by Chris

Under the auspices of the NAS there was a Beyond Barriers meeting set for Wednesday 18th October 2017 for students with disabilities at the university. Owing to a clash of dates, Chris was not able to attend this first meeting so the detailed scope and intent of this particular meeting are not known.

As a result of one of his similar meetings with Rachel (NAS), Chris prepared what essentially amounted to a list of his personal attributes:

Chris Thorpe –
Preparation for the Beyond Barriers Meeting –
Things I am good at:

- Data handling – data input and analysis

- Database and website design

- Working to deadlines

- Punctuality

- Reliability

- Categorising

- Working methodically

- Remembering facts

- Spotting errors

- Routine

- Working with spreadsheets (Advanced level?)

- Polite and kind

Weaknesses:

- Coding

- Tasks that require multiple paths

- Communication in group settings

- Scientific maths (strength is functional maths)

- Managing sudden change, without explanation

How my autism affects me:

- I sometimes feel the need to pace back and forth and flicker my hands when excited

- I have difficulty judging appropriate volume for my voice

- I struggle with tasks that require multiple paths, simultaneously
- I think and function in a logical way
- I have a warm body temperature
- I am a very positive and philosophical person
- I think literally
- Social communication difficulties – I may not always be able to judge the appropriateness of what I say in a social situation.

This summed him up well. It was rather like a concise self-portrait.

In December 2017, there was a constructive outcome to the earlier Beyond Barriers meeting that he had not been able to attend. Chris and other students with disabilities would now each be assigned a mentor for support in any way appropriate or needed. Great stuff. This would complement the work of the separately assigned supporter for his main project, as well as his weekly hour with Rachel.

It was apparent that he was benefitting from exposure to these Beyond Barriers ad hoc meetings. Because he positively blossoms with one-to-one interaction, there was no doubt that such meetings would definitely involve animated, two-way discussions, from which he would gain a great deal.

When his time at university is at an end, hopefully suitable conduits may be available for him within which to channel such interaction in the future and in whichever direction takes his fancy. It would be a shame if all he did after his studies was retire to his room in front of his beloved computer. Isolation is not the name of the game here.

He loves films and will go to the cinema at the drop of a hat.

Cinema holds a great interest for him and he also has a keen interest in factual TV and natural history.

He watched the first couple of episodes of the first series of *The A Word* which was a BBC family-based TV fictional drama about an autistic youngster, but found little interest in following the story and retired upstairs. It appeared he got little benefit from it.

Dad and Mum had watched the complete first series of *The A Word* and sat down to watch the first episode of the second series broadcast on BBC in November 2017. The end of the first episode was as far as they got. This led to some interesting conversations between them but with both protagonists actually on the same side of the argument.

The first question essentially involved a rather basic premise.

"Why are we actually watching this?"

They readily acknowledged they already watched more TV than they really should ("Blame sport", says Mum). Leaving aside the always watchable Christopher Ecclestone, the script felt rather politically correct. It was not so much to do with autism but rather more based upon the reactions of others within their own relationships, in and around the subject of autism. A not unnatural basis for a drama-based piece of television but, of course, autism has direct relevance to Chris and his parents. The emotional scenes in relation to the autistic child appeared rather contrived. Sorry – but that's just how it felt.

One aspect of this episode particularly grated. Leaving a ladder up to a school roof once might be understandable – twice would just not be allowed to happen. There appeared to be less to learn about the autist but too much concentration on the independent lives of those about him. It was difficult to empathise with the child's parents who appeared rather too keen to attempt to make him 'normal'. The father acted like a prat whilst the mother was in denial. Again, sorry – but that's just how it felt.

★★★

Delivery date…pending

Chris came home one evening in November 2017 concerned about the nature of a conversation he had had with his lecturer, regarding the content of his latest submission for his Digital Business module. She had apparently said on the Monday that the submission he had already made for marking in advance of the Friday drop-dead date was not what was wanted – it was wrong.

He had evidently had problems trying to explain to her the basis of his planned submission for the Friday. He had produced a whole series of presentations for marking and had shown her the extent of the draft work. The only problem was that they constituted the wrong submissions at this time.

Chris had effectively prepared a full business plan submission, when what was actually wanted at this stage was only a basis (or precis) of a prospective 'pitch' to investors related to his hypothetical new online business.

In spite of his tremendous progress in almost every respect related to his autism, once again this was an example that, no matter how much things may change, certain things stay the same.

Chalk and cheese. They are both appropriate in their individual respects but different they most certainly are. This situation was akin to him going round the M25 when, in practice, he should have been heading down the M3. Where's that satnav when you need it?

Chris had otherwise been coping very well with the needs of university life and his modules without direct intervention being required by the family. Mum would usually have been the first to act in terms of reminders and the like anyway. Here was one particular instance though where intercession was appropriate. Yes…he had got the wrong end of the stick.

A parental email enquiry happily brought explanation, clarification, support and confirmation of an understanding of Chris's situation by return. From the outline of the written scope of the work to be done, it was evident that Chris had tried to run before he could walk and had actually done too much. The tutor had apparently been talking to Chris in the guise of someone on the receiving end of a presentation, saying what was wanted, where, when, how and why, and perhaps appearing to be rather forthright in her delivery (role play acting in fact).

Again, autists, even high-functioning ones like Chris, have virtually no means of analysing, recognising, interpreting or understanding body language. Here was a classic example of him patently misinterpreting the play-acting being portrayed. Dad and Mum had some success in pointing out what had happened and he was content, with the understanding now in place. He knew the bare bones of what was wanted.

The tutor was prepared to give an extension to the drop-dead date for delivery of the piece which was a much appreciated offer. It then transpired that Chris made the submission by the original Friday deadline anyway without further reference or discussion, being apparently quite happy with what he had given in to be marked.

So, what was the outcome of this little hiatus? He was as pleased as punch to be able to announce one evening that "The scores are in!" He had received a mark of 66% for this aspect of the work. Not only that but this 66%, as he was even more pleased to impart, represented 35% of his total marks for this whole module, one of the four modules for this final year of study. With some knowledge of the extent of the additional work already done by Chris at this stage, great comfort was drawn from the thought that there was a more than even chance he might gain the level of a 'pass' for this module.

Just before the Christmas break, Chris was called upon to present an outline, a 'pitch' if you will, of the basis of his Final Year Project. As robots featured high in terms of his interests, this was not going to be too much of a challenge. He would have to be suitably forearmed and forewarned before the event, thus revision, planning and preparation were required. Chris intended to be properly prepared. The marks for this work were to represent 5% of the total marks available for the module. Now, this is not such a high proportion of the overall marks, but he was able to confirm that he got 66% marks for his presentation.

It appeared he was beginning to get higher marks for aspects of his work. Improvements, greater understanding, further development or just natural evolution? Who knows? Time would tell.

Everyone is changed by circumstances in life and impacted by their experiences. How then might it be possible to define and measure progress? By school, college or university exam marks, by course work, marked results or even by the simple expedient of observation. However, all such measurements, whilst not actually arbitrary, are rather subjective in that the yardstick has already been set in each case and individuals are just compared to these predetermined parameters, or notches on the yardstick.

The degree of success or progress remains a variable measure but Chris has progressed nonetheless. Measurement of progress by attainment of exam results is only a constituent in the proper development of children and young adults, especially those with disabilities.

Chris's concerns, such as they are, are never far from his mind. As has been said before, he is increasingly capable of vocalising such concerns, usually at speed, which means he can sometimes stumble over his word output until he takes his foot off the verbal accelerator. He finds sharing these thoughts increasingly rewarding. He has so much to say and so much he wants to understand. He is always concerned to try to do the right thing.

He has been doing some further personal development activities closer to home. One of these is for him to take the bus in the village on his own into town, there to be met at the other end for drinks, shopping and the like. So far this has worked out fine and the family have not lost him yet. Repeating this exercise will embed the routine, reducing the risk factor more and more each time. Other bus trips could follow...anything to broaden his mind, outlook and experience of life and this should continue to support his growing independence.

Routine still figures high in Chris's make-up but by now he is not so much a slave to it and it may be that he uses it rather more to mark his own progress through the day.

To see him now at the age of twenty-five reading fiction books, although mainly associated with his current games-related interests, is a delight and, to a mother who was apparently born with a bookmark in her crib, a real joy.

"Never thought we would live to see the day," she says.

When parents are lucky enough to have a child, there is a school of thought that says this involves a specific, challenging choice. Have they been given a block of wood to carve into a recognisable and pre-planned shape or a young sapling to feed, nurture, cultivate, observe, care for, support, help and then marvel at the end result? Dad and Mum, given the choice, would say with quiet conviction that they were very much in the sapling and nurturing camp.

Chris is turning out to be a rather special young man, definitely his own man, and this is as it should be. However, he is not yet at the end of his road – far from it.

CHAPTER TWENTY-EIGHT

How He Will React

Chris is a WYSIWIG type of person (What You See Is What You Get). He is very happy in his own skin and does not generally miss the sort of social interaction many regard as essential to add a little colour to the way life is lived.

He gives every outward impression of being laid back and phlegmatic, but to take the swan analogy, what you see may well not be representative of what is actually happening below the water line. He is particularly sensitive to, and aware of, 'atmosphere' and if there is any sense of tension or conflict he will cut straight through it explicitly.

"Is everything all right?"

Chris will say what he sees. The inference might be that he is not blessed with tact, although by any reasonable measure of accuracy, it may well be that he is voicing the pure unvarnished truth. It has been seen in many cases that he is not entirely tactless. He will sometimes, almost deliberately, pause to think before he speaks. He is, however, totally guileless.

Many years ago on the occasion of a visit to the home of Godfather, Michael, when the good gent had a lighted cigarette in his mouth, Chris turned round and said:

"Smoking is bad for your health."

"Quite right, Chris," came the response.

It was, of course, the plain truth delivered in Chris's unself-conscious style, directly and without fear of recrimination. In exactly the same situation many years later, and with his now well-developed sense of irony, he would deliver the same line but with a twinkle in his eye and an early laugh. In neither case would he have demanded any reaction either way from the recipient, he would be simply stating a fact as he saw it. So it might be said that Chris has opinions but does not necessarily have the need to assign judgement.

Mum, like most of her gender, has refined shopping into an art-form. ("Careful, careful...dangerous ground here," says Dad.) Chris will ask if he can buy items for himself online, or go off and explore, and buy something of his own choosing when out shopping. He well understands the cost of things and has no problem at all managing a budget.

A feature of Chris's make-up is whether he actually understands the concept of value. At home he will always ask if he can spend a specified amount of his own money online even when the cost of such a purchase might be quite modest. The thought occurs that this is out of courtesy rather than anything else as good manners are so instilled in his demeanour. He is by no means profligate – caution is his byword.

Finger on the pulse

Chris had never cut his fingernails. He always bit them. This was not through any perceived sense of anxiety, but Mum made him a proposal. If he stopped biting just two of his fingernails for two weeks she would give him £2. This was to see if he would appreciate the difference it could make for his fingers when he saw the results.

He waited the allotted two weeks before presenting the results to Mum, but this was to be on the basis of actually not biting any of the nails on his hands at all. Yes, it had made a real difference already to how his hands looked, and he was now in a position to trouser £10 rather than just the £2. Creative accounting at its best.

A concentrated mind

In the film comedy, *Miss Congeniality*, William Shatner plays a seedy beauty pageant host and in one scene asks a range of banal questions to vacuous beauty queen contestants. Sandra Bullock is the heroine, playing a character not actually vacuous, but in the pageant as part of the plot, and remembers to answer:

"World peace," when asked what she would like above all else.

A trite response to a trite question.

Dad has taken this one step further when out and about and occasionally, when asked the supplementary question by a sales assistant or waitress:

"Is there anything else, sir?"

"World peace," would be the reply, just to see what the reaction would be.

Thankfully there is usually a humorous exchange and he has yet to have the need to extract his nose from the soup. The slight problem for the family is that Chris has taken up this attribute rather enthusiastically, though laughing as he says it, just to be sure his intent is not misconstrued. Bless him.

Rather engagingly, in the summer of 2017, he suddenly enquired:

"Where's Camelot?"

Now there is a quandary which even to the current day is not easily reconcilable. You try it!

Chris does not worry about things, but he can remain concerned about current affairs and the content of the news on the television. He does find it hard to understand how people can be so inconsiderate of each other.

He is concerned with the vagaries of the human condition in the sense of his incredulity at the pain, anger and tone of all conflicts often represented in the media. His ideal would be for everyone to live in peace, on a level playing field. It cannot be denied that this is an ideal harmonic objective, but it has been pointed out to him that there are always peaks and troughs and hills and gorges on that path. To try to explain to him why people do bad things to others is not an easy task.

Given a choice between good and evil, Chris will choose good over evil every time. It's a bit of a Forest Gump thing really. Chris is pleased when Dad and Mum have been able to flesh out the situation around a set of circumstances which can be said to represent good news, then to be able to go on to develop possible future constructive or satisfactory impacts from that good news.

He is most interested in trying to make sense of politics. To which the parental observation is that he is no different to so many people in that quest. It may take a very long time to get the sort of answers he is looking for and what he sees on the news forms the basis of extensive conversations at home. If it was up to him, there would always be a solution. This is the ultimate conflict for him when it is explained that politics and religion very rarely present the opportunity for a black or white, yes or no, satisfactory and mutually agreeable solution.

As far as religion is concerned, he has a varied and deep interest in both science and science fiction. How this relates to religion for him really boils down to wanting to live in peace with his fellow man and when he is no more, believes he will simply slide off into one or more of the parallel universes as part of the multiverse.

When out and about in supermarkets, shops, or restaurants,

Chris makes a particular point of reading the name-badge of the person serving, and if there is no badge, he will unabashedly ask for the person's name. It is usually a way of starting a conversation, but does appear to be a consistent trigger in his make-up.

He has the ability to identify and demonstrate to others an interest in current affairs. He can be quite direct in his support for something he has seen reported on the news or on the internet, and conversely, not at all shy in expressing strong concern and disagreement with perceived injustice.

He could do with a parrot on his shoulder as a sort of universal moderator. Dad and Mum are able to fill in some of the wider context to these situations and this has led to some quite involved conversations.

Chris has taken on board that, when it comes to politics and religion, there simply are no actual answers. It is quite right and proper, however, to have an opinion, to share it and discuss it – this is part of the process.

He is inquisitive by nature and intent. However, there is some doubt that he could ever be an economist because if you put twelve economists together in a room you would probably get thirteen points of view. Chris would be infinitely more direct.

Dad and Mum have always tried not to say a straight no to Chris, but rather outline to him the possible consequences of his actions and decisions, and giving him the freedom to make a considered choice.

He has a strong sense of justice and right and wrong. On one famous occasion, when he was much younger, he literally sprang into action to attempt to provide the physical means of Thomas being able to regain possession of certain rare Pokémon cards. These cards had been misappropriated during a visit to the family home by someone who, up until then, had been considered a friend of Thomas.

Fortunately Dad and Mum were able to diffuse the situation

by the use of intense but measured language directed towards the discredited visitor who, rather miraculously, was then able to proffer the missing cards, without escalation of the exercise into overt physical intimidation.

Taking the lift with Chris...a trip into the unknown...or the inescapable

Conventionally, people get into a lift for the purpose of going up or down in this form of mobile box, with or without the company of others. Parental knowledge of Chris, however, indicates that the best way to travel in a lift as a family is, for them, on the basis of sole occupation. This, ideal, rather selfish, though prudent intent, is not always conveniently achievable. Consequences may ensue.

Busy places have other members of the public intent on their own travels and activities so joint occupancy of lifts will often occur. Even large lifts necessarily are of defined capacity. This may or may not place one closer to a complete stranger or group of people than one might ideally choose. Body language is not an exact science, of course, though much research has been done into this aspect of human interaction.

What cannot be denied, is that in such confined spaces as lifts, and generally being devoid of any choice in the matter of one's fellow travellers unless the lift is already full, the human receptors are at maximum sensitivity. Thoughts passing through the mind before any language arises may be along the lines of are they a threat? Are they likeable? Are they nice or not nice? Are they selfish regarding the space they appear to need? Are they noisy? Are they open to acknowledge anyone else? Are they...?

The standard lift etiquette at the reaction level is thus generally to do nothing and await developments.

Chris, however, has an entirely different and well-established lift etiquette. To the present day he will loudly greet incomers in a totally uninhibited fashion.

"Hello my fine friends. Welcome aboard."

If this gets no reaction to speak of, he will try further forms of direct invitation to communicate, but always with his characteristic best behaviour and politest delivery.

1) To the foreign lady wearing a sari and accompanied by her children, he says:

"Have you come from India to shop?"

2) To the patently partially sighted lady searching for the lift floor button:

"What's the matter, are you blind?"

Sounds much worse than intended, but there was no inflection in his voice, merely a possible statement of fact as he saw it. No offence intended, and fortunately none taken.

3) To the overweight woman:

"Are you pregnant?"

He may not be a candidate for the diplomatic corps, but he remains resilient, irrepressible and uninhibited. Above all, he is literal. He speaks as he perceives.

At such times Dad and Mum will look for some form of escape from the box. Waiting for the ground to open up is an impracticable solution when so suspended.

With regard to an earlier observation, Chris is not blessed with the ability to fully read and comprehend body language in the sense that others would understand. It's what he is – it's what he does. Happily to date, certainly when in company with the family, there have been no unfortunate reactions to such situations.

Frustration…not the game…real life

How does Chris cope?

Early one weekday morning in January 2018, Dad caught a snippet on the radio relating to a number of children having been excluded from school for one reason or another. In one case, a boy was reported to have been pulled back on the arm by his PE teacher, whereupon the boy responded by hitting the teacher on the shin with his hockey stick. That might have been the end of it, because there was little further discussion about the rights and wrongs of the case. The pupil had just been put on suspension.

This was what would conventionally be described as an open-and-shut case. The rather sad thing about this report though, was that right at the end of the piece, the boy was described as being Asperger's on the autistic spectrum. To those in the know, this could have put a whole different slant on the article, but there was no real clarification of the possible impact of the boy's condition on his situation. An unsatisfactory conclusion thought Dad.

How might Chris have reacted? What Dad did know for certain was that he would not have responded in such a manner.

Chris had been in very close proximity to others on the autistic spectrum all through his formal education. There might have been occasions when he could have been expected to demonstrate similar copy-cat behaviour, to be considered disruptive, destructive, reactive or at the very least, unruly. There is no knowledge, recollection or report of any such event. Chris seems to have merely ploughed his own furrow through those stages of his life without the need to pick up such behavioural traits.

"How ever did he survive?" thought Dad.

When in the Supported Learning Unit at Brooklands College and therefore no older than eighteen, one of his college mates had a problem. Not just an ordinary problem, but a thumping really great big one.

Chris was in the IT room interacting with one of the computers on some aspect of his work. His friend came back into the room to find that someone else had sat down at the computer work-station he had been using. Well, to be fair, he always used that particular work-station and, no doubt, felt a degree of ownership towards it. Evidently he felt an insurmountable degree of frustration at this invasion of his work space and, in modern parlance, went right off his rocker. He was upset and inconsolable. Discretion being the better part of valour, and no doubt with input from the lecturer, the lad who had usurped this location moved on to another. With the situation resolved, Chris's friend resumed his seat having calmed himself down.

Chris related this story at home that evening.

"What would you have done in that situation, Chris?"

"I would just have used another computer," he said succinctly.

So, almost without thinking about it, he had solved a possible frustration problem for himself by not getting in that situation in the first place. Nice one!

One reaction Chris has at times of apparent frustration is to appear quiet or reflective when things don't seem to be working properly, or if he has something on his mind. How does he get out of this mind-set? It is usually by talking to Dad and Mum who try not to put doubts in his mind, simply offer a way of dealing with the situation.

Chris was asked what he would do when he found something or someone causing him frustration.

His response was along the lines that, where he might have a problem with one of his games, he would eventually put the game down and return to it when inclined to do so. As he saw it, this was the limit of his frustration level.

"I understand," said Dad. "It's good to know what you believe to be your highest level of frustration. I have to say I don't ever remember you throwing your toys out of the pram, Chris."

To which he responded:

"Daaaadd! – I didn't ever throw my toys out of the pram."

Dad was being humorous. The response from Chris was delivered as a statement of fact. Mind you, he did have that glint in his eye at the time.

Frustration does not appear to be a significant obstacle for Chris either in terms of management or reaction. He does something about it if he can or gets over it and moves on.

Uninhibited...again...and again

Whilst Chris was heavily involved with his *Robot Wars* final year project, he had an unexpected bonus in the form of the engaging, capable and most competent, Mr Dara O'Briain.

Not only was this good man the host for the *Robot Wars* TV shows but he was what can only be described as the most uninhibited host for the Go 8 Bit television show mentioned in Chapter Nineteen. These two shows ran on similar timelines though on different channels giving Chris full licence to let off steam in his own raucous, uninhibited, inimitable and noisy style twice for two different programmes.

The sofa rocked. Dad, having lost temporary custody of the television volume control, was wishing he had some ear-defenders (i.e. headphones or ear muffs). This would possibly have been of limited use anyway since Chris can now exhibit the same uninhibited reaction to anything of a similar nature which strikes his fancy. Long may it be so. Look out, world – here he comes.

Uninhibited…yet again

The Pirate Dinner Show in Florida has already been covered in Chapter Ten and there was another dinner show on that holiday which demonstrated Chris's tendency towards enthusiastic and uninhibited reactions. It was the Sleuth Dinner Show.

The format here was that there were some twenty-five tables, each of twelve or so place settings, in front of the raised stage. A cast of six or so actors then played out a murder mystery without a conclusion. The sit-down meal followed the first half of the show and Dad particularly remembers rib-eye steak as his main course and key lime pie as dessert, really not bad at all.

Enter the compere or host for the evening. His duties were to generally wind up the audience, cajole, harangue, entertain and keep the reactions coming thick and fast.

The purpose of this second half was for the audience to try and work out who was the perpetrator and the murder weapon used. Each table was to select a spokesperson to ask questions and try to solve the given clues.

With all the hullabaloo going on, the compere was re-running some of the options with cast members on stage and said:

"Everyone can see you."

To which Chris loudly voiced:

"Halloooo!"

Well – everyone seemed to laugh anyway.

CHAPTER TWENTY-NINE

How Will He React?

Chris lives in his own binary world but most definitely exists in the wider physical world. Just some of the challenges he has faced include colours, textures, relationships, philosophies, history, nature, cultures, geography, monuments, commerce, politics, religion, pain and joy. What Monty Python might refer to as The Meaning of Life.

Chris has an insatiable thirst for knowledge, facts, data and information. His cerebral hard-drive information interface retrieval system consistently proves that premise. He has his own moral compass, has definite views of what is right and wrong and is not shy to comment on articles which appear in any form of media.

He is very interested in space, not necessarily that which directly surrounds him, but that which is "out there", and a long way away...parallel universes and all that stuff. Limitless boundaries do not therefore present a problem for Chris but more of an opportunity for exploration and investigation. It may be that early exposure to the Cape Canaveral complex in Florida planted the seed and contributed to this interest.

Knowing how he will react, or parental thinking along the lines of "How will he react to this?" are not the same thing.

Despite all the trips made to Legoland with various adults, one was made on a slightly different basis. Thomas was left in charge of the house whilst the parents were away on a short break and planned that he and his mate would take Chris out for the day in the car.

They did not tell him the intended destination until they reached the turning off the main road leading to the Legoland site. Here Thomas was to learn the same lesson his parents had learnt much earlier with the Florida holiday, albeit with less histrionics. Chris was anxious and concerned all the time in the car. Of course he trusted his brother, but…!

Happily a great time was had by all and Chris was pleased to have been out with his brother and his friend. All inhibitions were reported to have disappeared on arrival, but again, it was a reminder of his difficulty in coping with a surprise, no matter how enjoyable it might turn out to be. No surprises please.

By his nature, it would be reasonable to describe Chris's reactions and responses as very literal. Is that entirely accurate? In June 2017, Thomas said that one of his model-army, game-playing contacts was currently a teaching assistant at Freemantles. In talking about the school, the family history and the school's new location in Woking, Thomas related a story which has relevance.

At the school, one of the pupils was asked to paint an apple. Not an unreasonable request, and indeed, the deed was done, although it was questionable that anyone would have wanted to eat it afterwards. The paper, however, remained pristine and untouched. That, surely, is being literal. Dad and Mum offer that Chris may not have been quite so literal.

It is accepted that Chris has identifiable characteristics. As a family, since Dad and Mum consistently and earnestly resist attempts to be categorised themselves, it is their particular wish that, whilst people may describe, analyse and relate to Chris, they should not categorise him. Classify him if necessary but do not categorise him. Do not put him in a box with a label.

Some views on Chris, based on who and what he is.

- Observant and inquiring.

- Interested and interesting.

- Trusting and trustworthy.

- Confident (and growing more so), but not arrogant.

- Aspirational (but not in the competitive sense), rather by the assimilation of knowledge.

- Resilient, resourceful and responsive.

- Exuberant, outgoing and irrepressible.

- Not born with a volume control.

- Lives very much in the present day, although accommodating the impact of future planned actions or activities can sometimes be a challenge.

- Exhibits exemplary time keeping.

- Will always try to do the right thing.

- Essentially incapable of being embarrassed or intimidated.

- Has a well-developed sense of humour. Irony features highly here.

- He remains on-topic and is not usually distracted from an assigned or chosen task until completion.

He has a most animated and engaging personality and at times can be rather effusive, though surely this is no bad thing. He will treat people and situations with an open mind and, unless previously encountered, with no particular preconceptions. He is keen to let people know his opinions and more than happy to listen to those of others. As has been said on many occasions.

"You never stop learning, Chris."

Dad and Mum say the same thing about themselves even at their age. So, how will he react? Spontaneously, without doubt.

Chris has always been an exuberant and uninhibited soul. One of his early cinema excursions circa 1998, was to see the film *A Bug's Life* whereupon, at the end of the film, he stood up and applauded enthusiastically, shouting:

"Bravo...Bravo!"

Dad...just being silly

Chris reacts totally without envy. He would no more envy someone anything than, well...fly to the moon. Like so many other attributes it is just not part of his make-up. The thought occurs that to some people envy is a sin. What is one of those anyway? Is it that a sin is something pleasant or unpleasant that you can pick up or put down as the inclination strikes? Or is it something to bang someone else over the head with, by way of trying to achieve a measure of superiority? Yes, it is another one of those ethereal concepts that Chris does not need to bother with.

Retribution, punishment, or divine delivery for what a sin might thought to be, is surely a pointless endeavour, since that requires one to be a judge and another to be a supplicant, whether willing or not.

Without dwelling further on the actual concept of judgement and on whom the responsibility for passing such judgement might reside, the question arises as to how Chris might be classified in respect of the Seven Deadly Sins. Would he be found wanting in that regard?

The Seven Deadly Sins are conventionally categorised as follows:

- Lust
- Gluttony
- Greed
- Sloth
- Wrath
- Envy
- Pride

Are these really sins or are they just characteristics of the person? Whether they are of themselves valid characteristics, or just matters of habit, or someone else's opinion, may well be a matter of prolonged discussion. Each person has some measure of these characteristics which, when taken together, serve to separate one person from another, either good or bad as the case may be.

Every system of measurement can be assigned an agreed tolerance by means of a percentage to account for errors and unquantifiable variables. Chris is not perfect by any means, so if a tolerance of, say, 10% is set in his case, the judgement needs to be made regarding to what degree Chris has any of these characteristics over a value of 10%.

Having studied Chris for many years, Dad would argue that, save for a maximum 20% value of not unnatural pride in his own achievements and, say, no more than 15% gluttony due to his predilection for pizza and salt and vinegar crisps, all other sins are at no more than the 10% level.

Within the limits of the analysis therefore, the proposition is that Chris's sin content be regarded as zero. All those who say 'aye', say 'aye'! This surely then puts him on a par with Mary Poppins, 'Practically Perfect in Every Way'. Not so sure about the skirt though.

Chris to act and react...or not

If this chapter serves to outline how Chris might act or react in future, there are certain behavioural traits he would not deem to be appropriate and to which he would not conform.

People are inclined to swear both in public and in private conversations – it is unavoidable – it is a fact of life.

Why do people swear? Some would say it is out of frustration or the desire for emphasis. Others may contend that it is because people are simply too lazy to think of a different, less confrontational set of words.

Unfortunately, there are also instances of anger, belligerence or loss of self-control which may have ongoing consequences over and above those appropriate to the circumstances at the time. In such situations, things can quickly escalate, even if considered to be under control by one party or the other. It is to be hoped that Chris would be able to avoid or deal with such cases of confrontation as and when they might arise. Most especially if that ire for one reason or another should be directed, rightly or wrongly, at him.

Chris does not swear and, as far as is known, has never exhibited the need for it. He does, however, become uncomfortable and concerned if he hears someone swearing and will normally attempt to adopt a tone of calming admonishment.

He never has, nor by any reasoned judgement, will ever have the need, to start smoking and would be able to outline in detail the health benefits to be had by not smoking.

Chris does not moan or complain – again, it is not in his nature to do so. His level of frustration, as far as his parents are concerned, would appear to be limited to that sometimes demonstrated round the dinner table. When discussing a matter in the news that all are agreed illustrates a point of concern or joint irritation, he may be minded to observe:

"Yeah – that really grinds my gears as well."

He will offer help and assistance where he can, but is he to be thought of as a paragon of virtue? Unlikely. Happily though, he may frequently be found to be intriguing.

There is a slight difference in emphasis between the titles of Chapter Twenty-Eight and Chapter Twenty-Nine.

Chapter Twenty-Eight – How He Will React

Chapter Twenty-Nine – How Will He React?

Chapter Twenty-Eight references certain of Chris's reactions to past events, circumstances, trials, tribulations and some of the enlightenments encountered during the various stages of his development. Many of these points can be said to identify him.

- Idiosyncratic...yes (without doubt).

- Intelligent...absolutely (without question).

- Decent all-round human being...yes (without hesitation).

Chris is observant, optimistic and matchless.

Chapter Twenty-Nine points to the future. Any assessment of how Chris will get on, and whether he will succeed or not, must remain subjective. His progress will continue to be followed with care, concern, commitment and no little hope. With this change of emphasis, there is the not unnatural contention that, how he will react, will fundamentally depend upon how he has done so in the past. There is, therefore, a firm belief that Chris's future will be based upon, and constantly display, a large degree of consistency.

By such means, he should be able to achieve continuity in his life to the satisfaction of himself and the advantage of others.

Chris gives every appearance of having approached his life to date with an open mind. In terms of being a follower, it would be fair to offer that he, as an ideal, has followed the provider of knowledge and information and then made up his own mind, on his own terms and as a result of his logical demeanour. Slavish adoration and contrite compliance are not his style.

Consideration of the contents of this book should lead to one's own conclusions, however so drawn. There are many other books out there. Go and seek your own knowledge since, hopefully, that way lies a measure of understanding and enlightenment for us all, no matter what the subject.

Decidedly, deliciously, devilishly ticklish

Chris is a lovely young man, a lovely character and a lovely soul. As has been said previously, he has what some call an 'invisible disability' but by no stretch of the imagination could he be described as being invisible.

He has come so far and achieved so much to date, but, by any reasoned assessment, he will go forward on the basis of being a credit to himself.

If you see him out and about, engage with him and you will get a warm and open greeting. He will talk about anything you want to talk about. He may well entertain you but he will certainly interest you. Walk towards him, try not to pass by on the other side.

...AND WHAT DID CHRIS THINK OF IT?

Well, the tale is almost told.

To get Chris's thoughts down in print might well involve an extent of content equivalent to that already laid down here. That is another story...

It was not the intent that he should be kept totally in the dark regarding all that has been written about him. In any event he will get to know of it soon enough. If he had been exposed to the full content of the book for an initial, detailed critique, although that would not have been a problem, this would effectively have ended up being a book about Chris, by Chris. Not the idea at all.

What has been done, however, is to get his feedback, good, bad, or indifferent, on the idea that it was thought important enough to write a book about him in the first place.

Rightly or wrongly he has no idea of...

- Just how *important* he is.

- Why it was thought *important* enough to lay out some of the steps along his autistic path.

- How *important* it might be that some others might derive value, direction, guidance, information, solace or reference from these stories, plus the inescapable entertainment and humour encountered along the way.

- How *important* it was that he came into the lives of Dad, Mum and Thomas.

It is self-evident that we are all similar to one another to some degree or another. Chris, by that same measure, by any measure in fact, is…totally…unique.

This chapter then gives the chance of a representative snapshot of his reaction to this parental request, entirely from his own perspective. His succinct and characteristically idiosyncratic script is written below, word-for-word, with editing limited to mere collation of the text into the given paragraphs for purposes of continuity and format. Enjoy!

QUOTE:…

I'd be honest, whenever someone wants to make a book all about me, I was surprised at first. After that, I am looking forward to see how this will turn out. You see, there are still some people in this world who are not aware of the term 'autism' which is sad if you think about it.

By publishing a book related to autism I hope it brings a spark of knowledge to all people. Therefore, they'll get along well with disabled people such as me. (Aside from one of the most embarrassing parts of my life. Thanks, Dad!!)

I've sure come a long way being in this world all thanks to my family and friends. I wouldn't be where I am, looking at the bright side of ideas and making others happy without them.

The world does need a lot of positive people nowadays. Like all people, we've all had our ups and downs but it all comes down to experience. Long ago during my early days, I used to get agitated with unexpected changes as they cause disruptions. That is until one day that had the most unexpected events in several hours, I was learning on how to cope with them.

It was quite interesting to see that it is very rare for a person with autism to attend university. That's what I've been told as I progressed. But now, that is changing as the staff members are doing what they can to support those with disabilities. For that, I was glad to hear.

Right now, I'm about to finish university and see if I can find myself a job using the skills and traits I've gained over the years.

UNQUOTE:...

... not a lot more to be said.

...AND DEAR READER

There is a lovely premise in the film, *The Most Exotic Marigold Hotel* ...

"It will be alright in the end.
If it is not all right now, that means we have not yet reached the end."

Second son Christopher, in the summer of 2018, will be twenty-six years old, hopefully fit, healthy and characteristically vocal. He will undoubtedly be autistic and may or may not be in receipt of a BSc (Hons) degree in Information Systems (Internet Business) from Kingston University in the UK.

Surely from his point of view it does not get better than that.

Whichever way his latest year at university goes makes no difference to who or what he is or has become, but his whole educational exposure and his evolution and progress to date has been fundamentally important to him and for him. Validation of what he has become.

Parental stress levels, particularly for his mother, in relation to his configuration as a human being, are happily now very much less than they were. Naturally though, the matter of Chris and his needs will continue to be a significant occupation in differing ways as time goes by.

As far as the immediate family (Dad, Mum and Thomas) are concerned and with the greatest thanks for the consistent and valued support of friends, acquaintances and remaining disparate relatives, we could not be prouder of him, nor more pleased for him.

By now you will have gleaned some insight into aspects of the life of a very special, engaging, ebullient and absolutely fascinating autist.

When Christopher came into our world, Mum, found herself to metaphorically be in Amsterdam rather than Paris. She moved on from there in due course. Chris will find his own destination, all being well.

Our autistic son beams brighter than ever.

... For Chris

Our autistic son

Our autistic sun

Walk on, walk on...

may you never walk alone

BEFORE YOU GO...

Dame "Steve"

Dad was driving home whilst listening to Radio Five Live when one of those interviews was broadcast which was of direct interest to him. This one struck a chord immediately and made him think back to earlier family discussions with Chris about what, not to put too fine a point on it, related to how to cope with certain physical needs.

The dulcet tones of Peter Allen introduced Dame Stephanie 'Steve' Shirley DBE, FREng, FBCS no less, a mature woman who came to the UK as a refugee many years ago. She gave the immediate impression of being a very strong character and was, and hopefully still is, a major philanthropist. Unmistakably highly intelligent, she had made a large amount of money from IT work (Information Technology). A very large amount of money indeed, having set up her own company to develop her work. Her overall story in the interview was absolutely fascinating – here was a very determined woman.

Unfortunately the interview was too long to be recalled in depth and in detail at the time because, of course, he was still driving on the motorway. It was not convenient to park up and concentrate fully on the interview. The nature of her earlier exposure to the autistic environment was therefore similarly sadly lost at the time. (Dad subsequently found out that her autistic son, Giles, died in 1998 at the age of thirty-five.)

She (Steve) now expends her energy in supporting IT but especially in relation to how it impacts on autistic people. She had set up her own ASD (Autistic Spectrum Disorder) school called Prior's Court and here was the very point of the interview. She contends that robots have a big role to play in helping even the most severely affected ASD people.

She said: "Robots do not instruct, they show."

Meaning that on a one-to-one basis they can repeat and repeat until a measure of knowledge and understanding is passed on, without any aspects of emotional censure or judgemental baggage or qualification. Without being too obtuse here, it is hoped that as in the case of our learning autists, you have likewise 'grasped the nettle' so to speak. This covers all bodily functions and needs.

Discussion on the radio turned to the matter of there also being some software for severely ASD people, where the individual can electronically press a green, orange or red button to indicate how they are feeling if they are stressed. A not unreasonable attempt to allow even the most challenged of autists some means of trying to express themselves as to the degree of their anxieties.

Experiments are apparently being undertaken to see the extent to which robots might usefully be able to have emotions or at least be able to offer empathy with this rather intangible concept. The matter of such robots was raised with Chris on the basis of thinking about the way in which they might be able to help from an educational, repetitive and non-judgemental set of circumstances. He found this talk markedly interesting in that expressive and excited way he would react when intrigued by a subject.

His response to this robot discussion was to say that if robots had feelings and empathy, they would be the same as him.

"Hello! – Hello!" the family thought. "He's not wrong there."

More help on tap

Another radio broadcast presented the story of an autistic child who was most reluctant indeed to take a bath and was demonstrating that reluctance with some vigour. The mother had tried many and various ways of achieving such an immersion, but to no avail. Enter, the Cat in the Hat, or more correctly, the Cat in the Bath. (That Dr Seuss has a lot to answer for.)

The cat did no more than jump up and land right in the bath water. No sooner had this happened than this dear child slid into the bath himself, all signs of distress and pique evaporating in the moment.

The question has to be asked…

"Why?"

Autists do sometimes need an outside influence to get to the next step in their reasoning process. The hope was that this was not just a one-off success in getting the child to have a bath. The activity should now be something learnt, experienced and part of his knowledge base.

The cat was no doubt a Maine Coone cat and therefore very happy to be in water. Chris can claim knowledge of such cats, and their characteristics, by virtue of next door's moggy at home.

Still growing

Wikipedia gives some wonderful quotes by Dr Seuss, which could be said to have particular relevance to Chris and those like him. They offer a great outline of positive mental attitude.

1. *You have brains in your head. You have feet in your shoes. You can steer yourself any direction you choose.*

2. *Be who you are and say what you feel, because those who mind don't matter and those who matter don't mind.*

3. *The more that you read, the more things you will know. The more that you learn, the more places you'll go.*

4. *You're off to Great Places! Today is your day! Your mountain is waiting,*

    so...get on your way!

5. *It's not about what it is, it's about what it can become.*